BLACK
STUDENTS

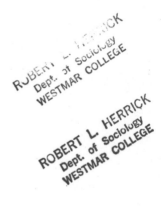

Harry Edwards $\boxed{Fp}$ *New York:*

BLACK

The Free Press   *London: Collier-Macmillan, Limited*

STUDENTS

The Free Press
A Division of The Macmillan Company
866 Third Avenue, New York, New York 10022

Collier-Macmillan Canada Ltd.,
Toronto, Ontario

Library of Congress Catalog
Card Number: 79-116809

printing number

1   2   3   4   5   6   7   8   9   10

*This book is respectfully dedicated to
the memory of Sammy Younge, Jr.,
James Chaney, Andrew Goodman,
Michael Schwerner, and the Black
students who died at Orangeburg,
South Carolina, in the sincere faith that,
by their sacrifices, they have contributed
greatly to the birth of a new dawn of
freedom, justice, and equality
in a new America.*

I would like to express my sincerest appreciation to the following people without whose unselfish contributions of time, ideas, and patience this book could not have been written. First, I am greatly indebted to Mr. Wil Mangas, Free Press' editor *sans pareil*, who again demonstrated his usual editorial brillance in criticizing and offering constructive changes while the manuscript was being developed.

My deepest gratitude also to Mrs. Nancy Wyatt, who painstakingly typed the manuscript in both its preliminary and, partly, in its final form.

A word of acknowledgment is also due my lovely fianceé, Miss Sandra Boze, who provided moral support when there arose the inevitable frustrations inherent in any attempt to develop three years of participant observation and semi-structured records into a coherent manuscript.

And may I express the boundless sense of pride and camaraderie I feel toward the present generation of Black Students. For me, Black Students have vindicated a deep faith I have in young people as the only real hope for the eventual establishment of freedom and justice in this society.

Finally, I would like to thank the Viking Press for permission to quote from H. Rap Brown, *Die, Nigger, Die;* Prentice-Hall for permission to quote from Andrew Billingsley, *Black Families in White America;* and Freedomways Associates for permission to quote excerpts from Lowell P. Beveridge, "Racist Poisons in School Books."

HARRY EDWARDS

Acknowledgments

On Malcolm X

Introduction

Contents

Before beginning the book, it seems appropriate to me to add a selected bibliography relating to the philosophy and life of Malcolm X, saint and prophet, who more than any other man first commanded Blacks to rise from their knees and assert their identity and racial pride.

Books

Breitman, George, *Last Year of Malcolm X, The Evolution of a Revolutionary*. New York, Merit, 1967.

Clarke, John H., ed., *Malcolm X, The Man and His Times*. New York, Macmillan, 1969.

Cleaver, Eldridge, *Soul on Ice*. New York, McGraw-Hill, 1968, pp. 50-61.

Epps, Archie, *The Speeches of Malcolm X*. New York, Morrow, 1968.

Randall, Dudley, and Burroughs, Margaret B., *For Malcolm*. Detroit, Broadside, 1966.

Warren, Robert Penn, *Who Speaks for The Negro in America?* New York, Random House, 1965.

Articles

"Malcolm X," Lawrence and Richard Henry, *Now*, March-April, 1966.

"The Malcolm X Myth," Albert Cleage, Jr., *Liberator*, June, 1967.

"Malcolm X The Martyr," Clarence Major, *Negro Digest*, December, 1966.

"Playboy Interview: Malcolm X," *Playboy*, May, 1963.

"Malcolm X: The Final Interview," Roland Miller, *Flamingo*, Ghana Edition, June 1965.

On Malcolm X

"Malcolm X Is Alive," R. A. Schrath, *America,* April 22, 1967.

"Violent End of a Man Called Malcolm X," Gordon Parks, *Life,* March 5, 1965.

"Minister Malcolm: Orator Profundo," N. H. Boulware, *Negro History Bulletin,* 1967.

"Tragedy of Malcolm X," *America,* March 6, 1965.

"Malcolm X: Nothing But a Man," W. T. Walker, *Negro Digest,* August, 1965.

"Brother Malcolm and The Black Revolution," W. Keorapetse Kgositsile, *Negro Digest,* November, 1968.

"The Legacy of Malcolm X," Betty Shabazz, *Ebony,* 1969.

"A Visit with The Widow of Malcolm X," Fletcher Knebel, *Look,* March 4, 1969.

BLACK
STUDENTS

End of a sit-in, Nashville, Tennessee,
February, 1960 (UNITED PRESS INTERNATIONAL PHOTO).

Black Student demonstration, Southern
University, March 1960 (UNITED PRESS
INTERNATIONAL PHOTO).

Birmingham, Alabama, May, 1961 (CHARLES
MOORE FROM BLACK STAR).

Malcolm X in Egypt, 1964 (JOHN
LAUNOIS FROM BLACK STAR).

Stokeley Carmichael (UNITED
PRESS INTERNATIONAL PHOTO).

Eldridge Cleaver and wife Kathleen, 1968
(S. SHAMES FROM BLACK STAR).

H. Rap Brown (UNITED PRESS INTERNATIONAL PHOTO).

Howard University, March, 1968 (UNITED PRESS
INTERNATIONAL PHOTO).

Carmichael and Brown at
Columbia University,
April, 1968 (TED COWELL
FROM BLACK STAR).

Northwestern University, May, 1968
(UNITED PRESS INTERNATIONAL PHOTO).

San Francisco State College, December,
1968 (UNITED PRESS INTERNATIONAL PHOTO).

Brandeis University,
January, 1969 (UNITED
PRESS INTERNATIONAL PHOTO).

University of California, Berkeley,
February, 1969 (ALAN COPELAND FROM
BLACK STAR).

Oberlin College, February, 1969 (UNITED
PRESS INTERNATIONAL PHOTO).

Cornell University, April, 1969 (UNITED
PRESS INTERNATIONAL PHOTO).

Queens College, June, 1969 (ST. CLAIR
BOURNE FROM BLACK STAR).

Few phenomena have struck the American educational system with the force of the present phase of the Black student movement. And few developments in American education have pointed up the potential for positive non-violent change—not only in the educational arena, but in the society at large—while simultaneously fostering an atmosphere filled with the language of revolution and of violent social and political upheaval. It is these divergent potentialities which make the present phase of the Black student movement a prime subject for exploration and analysis. Furthermore, as a highly seminal reality of modern American life, the dynamics of the movement must be understood if an important step toward social, economic, and political justice in America is to be taken.

The Black student revolt did not start with the highly publicized activities of the Black students at San Francisco State College in California. The roots of the revolt lie deeply imbedded within the history and structure of the overall Black liberation struggle in America. The Black student movement had its beginnings in the idealism, ingenuity, and just plain guts of young Black men and women who were attending southern negro colleges in the late 1950's and early 1960's. It was these students who provided America, for the first time in its history, with a major social movement both initiated by and led by young Afro-Americans.

Although the slogans, philosophy, and methods of the movement have undergone several changes—as have these aspects of the freedom struggle in general—the goals of the movement have remained singularly unchanged. The same freedom, justice, and equality sought by the young Black students who non-violently endured the brutality of southern racists during the sit-ins of the early 1960's is the same freedom, justice, and equality sought by Black students who are today calling for "All Power To The People, and Black Power To Black People—By Any Means Necessary." For, Blacks—especially young Blacks—have never confused means

Introduction

with goals. The goals are, and always have been, absolute and immutable. Only the means and language have changed. Freedom is freedom, whether gained through integration or separation. Justice is justice, whether achieved within an integrated neighborhood or within the structure of a separate Black community. And, an equal opportunity for the pursuit of life, liberty, and happiness is an equal opportunity regardless of whether it is achieved by holding hands with white folks and singing "We shall overcome" or by force of threat, disruption, or premeditated violence. The Black student movement, then, has progressed from the naiveté of the "integrationist" oriented phase of the movement in the early sixties, to the present phase with its emphasis on "Freedom By Any Means Necessary." The experiences that have led young Afro-Americans to embrace this change have been both valuable and costly. Thousands among this present generation of young Blacks have witnessed and withstood the brutality inflicted upon them and their white allies on the picket lines at Hattiesburg, Mississippi; the damp, filth-infested jails in Alabama, Georgia, and Arkansas; the electric cattle prods, high-powered fire hoses, and the hardwood clubs and bayonets of the police and the military, both down north and down south. And, based upon their evaluations of the cost-achievement ratio produced by these sufferings, today's students have decided that new approaches to the old problems of racism and injustice are both desirable and needed. So, in the space of a decade, Black student activists and protesters have gone from the espousal of a political strategy based upon the religious notion of redemptive suffering to an adamant belief in and advocacy of the strategy of creative disruption. And as we enter the decade of the 70's we are apparently witnessing the emergence of a strategy of retaliatory violence.

The present phase of the Black student movement—like the earliest manifestations of the revolt—took the more traditional negro civil rights organizations, such as the N.A.A.C.P., by surprise. However, given the impatience of young Blacks with the snail's pace of integration, their ever increasing race pride and self-awareness, and the increasingly greater popularity and appeal of the more radical and revolutionary philosophies and means, the changes which have come about in the Black student movement were both inevitable and, to some extent, predictable.

My central task in this book is to present the historical development of the Black student movement—the factors underlying the emergence and waning of its various phases; the characteristics and philosophies of the movement's present participants; and its possible future directions. I also will discuss numerous other aspects of the movement, among which are: the estrangement of liberal white "allies" from the Black student movement and the potential for future Black-white coalitions; the relationships between Black student groups and "the Black community"; the relationships between Black students and American colleges and universities; institutionalized racism in American education; and the feasibility and legitimacy of developing functional and distinguishable Black curricula throughout all levels of the American educational system.

The contributions of white students to the freedom struggle in America I will take up only insofar as they relate directly to some aspect of the Black student movement under discussion. The intention here is not to ignore the parts played by white students in the fight for freedom, but to present, in as clear and specific a fashion as possible, the history, present character, and the direction of a facet of the liberation struggle in America which is being carried on by young Black students today. No sane person can, in all humanity, deny the sincerity and contributions of young white students, such as Andrew Goodman and Michael Schwerner, who paid with their lives for their activities in support of their belief in the basic human dignity and rights of all people. Nor can the contributions of thousands of other young whites be dismissed as insignificant. Such people regularly left the security of middle- and upper-class white neighborhoods in the north, what was, at the time, the tranquility—and sterility—of northern colleges and universities, and the comforts of sun-drenched beaches and summer resort areas, to risk their lives attempting to register voters and desegregate buses and lunch counters in the south. However, as I stated above, the central concern here is the analysis and clarification of the past contributions, the present activities, and possible future role of Black students in what can be defined not only as a Black liberation struggle, but as a human rights struggle. For not only do the futures of Afro-Americans hang in the balance, but those of all Americans. Hopefully, by accepting this fact, we will achieve a greater understanding of an ostensibly regressive, aberrant, and chaotic aspect of one facet of a contemporary American social movement. If there emerges, out of this greater understanding, at least a few new perspectives, and at least a willingness by those in positions of authority to attempt the new, the untried, and, perhaps, the heretofore unthought of courses of action that may alleviate some of the racism and injustice that afflict America, then Sammy Younge, Jr., James Chaney, Andrew Goodman, Michael Schwerner, and the Black students who were gunned down by racist cops in Orangeburg, South Carolina, shall not have died in vain.

THE SEEDS OF REVOLT: IDEALISM IN THE MIDST OF SYSTEMATIC OPPRESSION

Idealism and oppression are antithetical forces, diametrically opposed. To the extent that these two intangible, but powerful, phenomena exist within a single social-political milieu, then to that same extent the seeds of revolt germinate there. And unless one of these forces or the other is eliminated —not changed, but totally eliminated—the seeds ultimately and inevitably bring forth their bitter fruit—violent, revolutionary social and political upheaval.

One way of viewing both the origins of and the impetus for the Black student movement in America is as a life and death struggle between the inertia of almost four-hundred years of systematic Black oppression and the idealism of Black youth. Although certainly an oversimplification, this perspective does provide an intuitive "feel" for the framework out of which the Black student movement emerged and within which it was nurtured and continues to grow.

Despite disdain for the "bourgeois negro middle-class" so often expressed by contemporary participants in the Black student movement, the fact remains that it was the offspring of "bourgeois" negroes who were the primary initiators of the movement. Indeed, the overwhelming majority of militant young Blacks active in the present phase of the movement— as will be shown in a later chapter—are themselves products of the negro middle-class. As in any organized movement

Chapter 1

aimed at bringing about over-all social change on behalf of the masses, the initiators and prime participants in the Black student movement had to be close enough to the effects of oppression to be cognizant of their impact, yet far enough removed to realistically envision a better way of life. They had to be intellectually sophisticated enough to synthesize diverse and superficially unrelated characteristics of the social order and to understand these as part of a fabric of systematic oppression, and yet be mentally flexible enough to simultaneously communicate these systematic relationships in the form of social issues with which the masses could identify and around which they could be mobilized. And they had to have the perception, honesty, and courage to see themselves as victims of the hard realities of the Black experience in white America, and yet at the same time be sufficiently removed from those realities to retain and nourish the idealism that has served as the energy source from which they have drawn stamina and direction. In this society, the only class of individuals even remotely capable of consistently producing people with this combination of characteristics has been the negro middle class. Although individuals have emerged from all classes of Black society to play significant roles in the Black liberation struggle, it has been the negro middle class that has provided both the student movement and the larger struggle with most of the required brains and a disproportionate amount of the brawn.

I do not mean to convey the notion that the Black middle class constitutes a bastion of revolutionary dialogue, debate, and ferment. To the contrary, as E. Franklin Frazier showed in his classic *Black Bourgeoisie*, the exact opposite is quite possibly more accurate.[1] The negro middle class has historically been conservative, socially neurotic, and to a large extent pro-status quo, if not anti-Black, on many issues centering upon questions of racial injustice in America. How,

[1]E. Franklin Frazier, *Black Bourgeoisie,* New York, The Free Press, 1959.

then, has this class produced, in such abundance, individuals who are not only politically active, but who have initiated and perpetuated a movement having the potential of bringing about violent revolution on behalf of the masses?

The negro middle class

According to the accounts of many students of the Afro-American experience in North America, the historical heritage of the negro middle-class derives its character not so much from the brutality and hardships suffered by Black field hands in seventeenth-, eighteenth-, and nineteenth-century America as it does from the relatively privileged existence of mulatto "house niggers" during slavery. Even today, it is widely felt among many Black and white Americans that this history of having functioned in the "upper echelons" of slavery is chiefly responsible for the air of superiority exhibited by middle-class negroes in their dealings with lower-class Blacks. This, despite the fact that many middle-class negroes come from families which have been middle-class for only one or two generations. Clearly, there are factors other than differing historical advantages and experiences in slavery which make the perspectives and attitudes of middle-class negroes different from those of the masses of Afro-Americans.

If there is any segment in Black America which can be regarded as being not just in America but at least partially of it, in the sense that it has managed to at least partially realize some aspects of the "American dream" and conversely to escape some of the degradation that the Black masses have come to know as the "American nightmare," it is the negro middle-class. Middle-class negroes accept most of the values extant within the general society and, likewise, are similarly afflicted by many of the society's shortcomings. For in many cases, they have worked hard and deliberately to attain their status as middle-class negro Americans. Some members of this class can in fact trace their socio-economic heritage back to the relatively privileged existences led by their forebears as house servants on slave plantations or as free negroes during the slavery era, but most have gained their middle-class perspectives and life styles through their own blood, sweat, and tears or the struggles and hard work of their parents and grandparents. Many still can remember the horrors of ghetto living. Daily newspaper, radio, and television accounts of the effects of poverty on lower-class Blacks strike home only too clearly. For many of them feel that despite their apparent economic and social affluence they themselves are at most only one or two steps removed from that same hell.

But despite their ability to empathize with the plight of downtrodden and impoverished slum-dwelling Blacks, in the past few middle-class negroes have rallied to the cause of the masses. Rather, perceiving their own well-being as highly tentative, unproven, and fragile, they have typically withdrawn from the challenge, removing themselves physically, socially, and psychologically from the ghetto. Often feeling insecure about and protective of their newly won liberation from the shackles of abject poverty or traditional welfarism, they have exhibited, as a class, a steadfast refusal to become involved in racial controversy, usually suspecting, and not without some justification, that the level of existence that they enjoyed was maintained through the tolerance and sufferance of whites as much as by their own hard work. Thus, middle-class negroes have developed feelings of superiority toward lower-class Blacks while still burdened with deep-seated feelings of insecurity. The middle-class negro has, in the past, not only sought to put forth the notion that he is certainly better off, if not better, than the lower classes of Blacks, but he has also tried to forestall any social or psychological identification with the Black masses because of his own insecurities.

Astonishingly enough, many middle-class negroes today still manifest an anti-Black "hang up" over skin color. In these times when affirmations such as "Black Is Beautiful" and "I'm Black, and I'm Proud" permeate Black society, many among the members of the negro middle class not only voice a preference for lighter skin color (if not an aversion for darker skin tones), but, in their more candid moments, will boast of their kinship ties to white forebears who, or so it seems, always turn out to have enjoyed high status and position in the ante-bellum southern aristocracy. This exaggerated importance placed upon skin color is, today, less a value derived from the advantages formerly gained by having light-colored skin in a racist white society, than it is a manifestation of the psychological insecurities of some middle-class American negroes. Even many whites today expect Blacks from all classes and age groups to be militant, defiant, and overtly arrogant about and proud of their kinky hair and "Black" skin, whatever its hue may in fact be. Yet older, middle-class negroes, in particular, continue to cling to this vestige of an era when light skin, in and of itself, was an advantage, both inside and outside of Black society, because in doing so they succeed somewhat in fulfilling their need to feel separate from the Black masses, most of whom just happen to be dark skinned.

For some older middle-class negroes, who did not have the "good fortune" to be born "high yellow," other neurotic methods of thwarting the psychological insecurities resulting from living a marginal existence between Black and white America became increasingly important. Such values as an exaggerated emphasis upon light skin and the desirability of marrying a light-skinned individual and the development of puritanical family and sex standards serve to assure the dark-skinned middle-class negro that his position in American society is not as shaky and insecure as he feels it to be. By thus separating himself from the masses of Blacks, at least in his own mind, he gains greater psychological security. But one of middle-class negro America's major "hang ups" provided much of the impetus for the Black student movement. I refer to the middle-class negro's obsession with education or, more specifically, the earning of academic degrees as a means of establishing and maintaining social and economic status, and as a sign of "good breeding," "refinement," and "superior culture."

A college degree has traditionally provided the middle-class negro not merely with a "union card" that enables him to get a better job than Blacks from the lower classes, but also with a sanctuary within which he can feel safe from the humiliations and insults heaped upon most Black Americans by whites. The educational experiences gained while earning the degree also give him access to ideas that provide a mental escape from the physical, social, and psychological stagnancy of negro life in the United States. As long as the middle-class negro could display his hard-earned degrees and diplomas on his living room or office wall, he could dismiss the racially derogatory slurs and degrading treatment he received at the hands of whites as a manifestation of their ignorance. And, more important, he could do so reassured that he himself was not ignorant—as his academic credentials attested. His degree has also contributed in another way to his feelings of psychological security. It has served to further set him apart from the Black masses—and this function is extremely important to him. In his perceptions of himself, relative to the masses of Blacks, a college degree gives the older middle-class negro, in particular, a feeling of cultural superiority and refinement. But more important it provides—in his way of thinking—some compensation for an undesirable accident of birth—the fact that he was born Black in a white racist society where Blacks are relegated to the very bottom, socially, educationally, economically, morally. It is hardly surprising, then, that the middle-class negro has traditionally stressed the importance of educational credentials beyond a high school diploma.

Very few middle-class negroes have felt that their college and university degrees obligated them to work for the improvement of the lot of the Black masses. First of all, as we said, the middle-class negro has traditionally regarded a degree as a status symbol and union card, and has not had a primary interest in the intellectual skills to be gained through the educational experiences accrued while earning that degree. Second, he has not infrequently enrolled in courses of study which have had only marginal and indirect relevance and applicability to the problems of the Black community. This tendency is due, in part, to the fact that American colleges and universities, both negro and white, have not developed curricula aimed at generating solutions to the problems faced by Black people and in which one could major and earn a degree. But the tendency also arises from the character of the middle-class negro's quest for the degree. He has been so engrossed in obtaining the "piece of paper" that he has often chosen snap courses which offered him little academic and intellectual challenge. (In this connection, that which is irrelevant is also, not infrequently, much less difficult than that which is relevant.) In cases where he has successfully completed relevant programs in medicine, law, and dentistry (which stress practical knowledge rather than a liberal education), the middle-class negro professional has typically used his skills to further his own economic and social interests rather than the over-all interests of the Black community. (In fact a good case can be made for the assertion that negro professionals have a vested interest in maintaining the system of oppression faced by the black masses. This is particularly true as far as the practice of segregation is concerned. Undoubtedly many of these professionals would not survive in a highly integrated and competitive society.) The professional's demeanor toward the Black masses is due in part to his perspectives, discussed above, relative to his lack of identification with the plight of Blacks. But, it also stems from the racially biased nature of American education. In the case of middle-class negroes who have in the past become school teachers, this fact is particularly pertinent, as we shall see later on in this book.

So as a group the middle-class negro traditionally has not been involved directly in the quest for solutions to problems facing Black people in general. Neither has he used the relevant educational skills that he has been able to acquire to that end. In short, he has accommodated himself to the problems of racial injustice in America in order to counteract his own psychological, social, and economic insecurities. He has typically been the docile, unthreatening negro, whom white liberals have taken to lunch, or he has been the token negro at the front desk in the white-owned business, or in the predominantly white block or neighborhood, or in the overwhelmingly white social club. He has been the *responsible negro*, the *respectable negro*—never *just* responsible or *just* respectable. And, this inescapable fact has traditionally been his burden.

The middle-class negro has typically been the "house pet" of guilt-ridden whites, particularly liberals. Like a puppy or tabby cat, he has responded to their petting with docility. The middle-class negro has, in essence, been the stereotypical "white man's nigger."

The house cat spawns a roaring lion

Despite the neurotic character of life in middle-class negro America, it did provide the milieu which has nurtured the Black student revolt. Unlike the lower-class Black, the middle-class negro, as a rule, has provided his family with all the material necessities of life—and some which were not so necessary. His white-collar job and his reputation as a "responsible negro" have enabled him to obtain credit and loans when supposedly less "respectable" and less "responsible" Blacks could not even qualify to fill out a credit or loan application. To get a loan a person must have a steady job and be able to point to stable, long-standing community ties. Clearly, lower-class Blacks do not possess these qualifications. Virtually always they are unprepared, lack the skills, to compete for the more desirable and financially rewarding jobs in the society. Often they are newly transplanted from the rural

12

south to the urban north. Often they move about within the confines of several Black communities to avoid paying exorbitant rents for sub-standard housing.

The middle-class negro, then, like the middle-class white; has found it relatively easy to obtain credit, loans, and to qualify for installment buying. The availability of credit traditionally has enabled him to maintain a "front" of economic affluence, conspicuous and ostentatious consumption, and security, while, in fact, he often has been living far over his head.

When this "front" of economic affluence is coupled with the fact, mentioned above, that the middle-class negro has, in the past, removed himself physically, socially, and psychologically as far away from the realities of the Black experience in America as he possibly could without doing the impossible and changing his racial heritage, we have the crucial elements of the milieu within which middle-class Black youth is reared. Add to this the exaggerated emphasis that the negro middle-class has usually placed upon obtaining a college degree, and the conditions necessary for the germination of the seeds of revolt are ideal and complete.

Unlike their parents, middle-class Black youths today have never really experienced firsthand the grim realities of life in the hard-core Black communities of America. Middle-class negro parents take pride in the fact that they have been able to shelter their children from such experiences. Although middle-class Black youths have been subject to many of the same racist humiliations and degradations that haunt the lives of the masses of Blacks, oppression and racism have had a much lighter impact upon them. Most have never known material want. And marauding rats and roaches are things they have heard about but never seen in their homes.

It has been this insulation from most of the tangible effects of oppression which has created a generation of middle-class Black people who are and have been outspoken and aggressive on issues involving racial injustice whereas their parents were docile and accommodating, who are and have been proposing radical programs of social reform whereas their parents have proposed no programs at all or have voiced conservative and even reactionary sentiments regarding social change, and who have been the prime participants and perpetuators of a movement with revolutionary potentials whereas their parents have often been too insecure even to speak the word "revolution." For one does not fear that which he cannot imagine. And again, unlike his parents, middle-class Black youths, children of relative affluence, can no more imagine themselves descending irreversibly into the pit of abject poverty than they can imagine the finality and loneliness of life on a distant, cold planet. In short, they simply cannot entertain the possibility of irreversible negative changes in their social and economic status. Thus, to a great degree, middle-class Black youths do not manifest the neurotic behavior and orientational patterns that their parents have developed to protect themselves psychologically from such a fate.

The emphasis placed upon obtaining a college degree by the negro middle class is also a factor of tremendous importance in fomenting the spirit of rebellion among Black students in the 1960's. As we mentioned, older members of the negro middle class have looked upon a college degree as a symbol of cultural superiority, refinement, good breeding, and as a union card. Any education achieved in the process of earning that degree has typically been of secondary importance. This has been less the case with their offspring. Having had, by and large, neither to develop nor to use many of the psychologically protective mechanisms concocted by their parents because of the relatively insulated lives they have led, today's young Black college students have been able to take the educational substance of their college careers seriously. To them, the college degree is merely the end product of the educational process. The degree is secondary to the full development of their innate intellectual capacities. The perspectives resulting from middle-class Black youths' quest for intellectual development and their emphasis upon mastering the substance of the educational process have given rise to a new era of enlightenment unrivaled in the history of the interactions between Afro-American youth and American society.

Even after passage of the school desegregation act of 1954, the discriminatory recruitment policies of northern educational institutions and the relatively high cost of tuition and room and board still prevented middle-class negro parents from sending their children to prestigious, predominantly white schools in the north. (Only 2% of the continued enrollment of the 80 top rated colleges and universities in America is Black. Only an insignificant fraction of this 2% is from what are known as "hard-core ghetto areas.") But despite the fact that most middle-class Black youths have attended conservative negro colleges in the south, where efforts have been deliberately made to play down the realities of racial injustice and Black oppression, the discrepancies between what these young Afro-Americans learned and what they perceived as the realities of American society, particularly south of the Mason-Dixon line, was, for them, intolerable. In their youthful idealism, which had not been weakened by the realities of Black life in America, they felt it to be their responsibility to confront these hypocrisies. And, the south provided ample opportunity for confrontation. The system of "southern hospitality" makes it crystal clear from the outset that *all* Black people have a "place." No Black person is put in the position of not seeing the steam roller of racism until it has flattened him. The message is made crystal clear—to be Black is to be a nigger is to be Black. And from it flows one of the most oppressive, brutal, inhuman social systems the world has ever known. No Black is exempt, be he a relatively privileged middle-class Black college student or an impoverished, indigenous southern Black sharecropper.

So the lines of confrontation were drawn, the idealism of Black youth on the one hand pitted against southern, white, systematic oppression and racial injustice on the other. From the outset, it was clear that this was to constitute a life and death struggle between these two forces. But for young Afro-Americans in the early 1960's, there was no turning back. Their idealism had given rise to a hunger for total freedom, justice, and equality, which could not be sublimated or channeled off. Idealism, if not crushed or diminished, becomes an irresistible force, compelling its possessor to action. It becomes an inexhaustible energy source, providing both courage and direction. Such was the case with the Black students who initiated the Black student movement in the first years of "the turbulent sixties."

FROM IDEALISM
TO REVOLT

We hold these truths to be self-evident, that all men are created
equal, that they are endowed by their Creator with certain unalienable Rights, that among these are Life, Liberty, and the
pursuit of Happines.—That to secure these rights, Governments
are instituted among Men, deriving their just powers from the
consent of the governed,—That whenever any Form of Government
becomes destructive of these ends, it is the Right of the People to
alter or to abolish it, and to institute new Government, laying its
foundation on such principles and organizing its powers in such
form, as to them shall seem most likely to effect their Safety and
Happiness.[1]

So reads, in part, one of the most revolutionary and inflamma-
tory documents ever conceived and adopted by civilized mankind.

On February 1, 1960, four Black freshmen at A and T
College in Greensboro, North Carolina, took seats at a theretofore "whites only" lunch counter located in a Woolworth
store in the downtown section of that city, not knowing that
they were starting a movement that would soon take on the
proportions of a revolution. It was the impact of just such
passages as the one quoted at the beginning of this chapter
that fired the idealism of young Black students, such as David
Richmond, one of the four students who initiated the first
sit-in, that set off the confrontation between the idealism of
Black youth and systematic legal oppression. For unlike the
racist white "founding fathers" of the Untied States of
America, who hypocritically coined both the Declaration of
Independence and the United States Constitution while simul-

[1]The Declaration of Independence, 1776.

Chapter 2

taneously condoning the perpetuation of the most inhuman system of institutionalized slavery known to civilized man, young Black students in the early 1960's believed in and took seriously such statements explicitly stipulating the basic equality, human rights, and dignity of all men. From the fact of this sincerity and serious belief in such doctrines, it was a relatively short step to active revolt. But unlike many other social and political movements, the Black student revolt was not to start amidst the smell of gun smoke and rampaging masses of humanity, but with a dignified request for coffee by four young Black men seated atop stools at a segregated lunch counter in a southern American city.

The sit-ins

It was the sit-ins more than any premeditated and deliberately devised method of attack that provided the initial tactical thrust for the Black student movement. Drawing inspiration from the activities and accomplishments of the late Rev. Dr. Martin Luther King and the Black people of Montgomery, Alabama, in their struggle to desegregate bus transportation in that city, Black students at many southern negro colleges left the classroom to join the revolt. Both intellectually and politically aroused, these students found academic life frustrating and far too removed from the social struggle raging just beyond the doors of their colleges. So they exchanged college attire and tree-lined campus scenery for "soul clothes" and the tenseness of the atmosphere to be found at segregated dime store lunch counters that were under attack by young Black students determined to be served.

Initially, the long-range goals of the Black student revolt were unspecified and the tactic of sitting in was unproven. Indeed, it was not even clear whether such a tactic could break down segregated lunch counters much less achieve such amorphous goals as freedom, justice, and equality. But pursue their goals and employ their tactic they did, all the while

18

having in most instances only an intuitive grasp of the gravity, nature, and monumental proportions of the task which they had undertaken. This naiveté was to be short-lived. For as the movement attracted more and more participants and more and more battle fronts were opened, the overt repression and brutality meted out by white racists increased proportionately. In order to realistically prepare themselves for upcoming confrontations in the light of what had been experienced in the initial sit-ins, Black students had to consciously routinize their tactics and reassess the magnitude of the obstacles with which they were faced. In this regard, racist white citizens, court officials, and law officers in the south deserve, perhaps, at least as much credit as the students for making the sit-in a legitimate, effective tactic of civil disobedience. For it was their brutality and inhumane treatment of protesters which gave moral credence and substance to the religious notion of "redemptive suffering" which is the heart of non-violent civil disobedience.

In time, liberal whites—particularly young whites from northern colleges—as well as older Blacks joined the students' struggle. Through the news media, especially television, the sincerity and determination of the Black students and the brutality that they were suffering had been brought into the living rooms of America. An identification with the moral spirit of the movement brought liberal whites and theretofore non-active Blacks as well into the fray. Such people as Bob Moses, a Black Harvard graduate and mathematics teacher in Harlem; James Forman, a Black student studying French in the north; Candie Anderson, a northern white girl from Pomona College in California, then attending Fisk; and hundreds of others joined the struggle. So great and so significant was the impact of the first sit-in that twelve days after the Greensboro incident, over forty young Black and white students undertook to sit-in at that same lunch counter. Spontaneity and self-sufficiency were the hallmarks of the sit-ins. Students initiated them and carried them out without adult advice or consent. Only the spirit of the movement, the uniformity of the tactics utilized, and the fact that Black students were the prime initiators and participants served to unify the young rebels. There was, initially, no formal organizational structure or leadership hierarchy guiding student efforts. It was essentially for this purpose that the Student Non-violent Co-ordinating Committee (SNCC or "Snick") was organized.

SNCC: Its goals, its means, its organizers, and its members

The Student Non-violent Co-ordinating Committee emerged out of a conference organized by Ella Baker at Shaw University, a southern negro school, during the weekend of April 15-16, 1960. Unlike many of the other participants in the Black student revolt, Ella Baker was no novice in the field of organizing and participating in the Black liberation struggle. A middle-aged Black woman with a degree from Shaw University, she had previously come south to set up the first full-time Southern Christian Leadership Conference (SCLC) office in Atlanta, Georgia, and had served as its first full-time executive secretary. She had decided in late 1960 that the sit-in leaders should be brought together. By this time, the movement initiated by Black students had spread to over sixty centers of sit-in activity. Miss Baker requested that SCLC underwrite, financially, the cost of the conference. So, with eight hundred dollars of SCLC money, the prestige of Martin Luther King, the organizational genius of Ella Baker, and the courage and idealism of Black youth as its prime elements, SNCC was born.

As we mentioned, the essential function of SNCC was to co-ordinate the various segments of the student movement throughout the south. Its official purpose, however, was stated more in terms of the means to be utilized in the movement than in terms of the goals which the movement was aimed at achieving. The first paragraph of the newly founded organization's statement of purpose served to set the theme for SNCC's activities in these initial phases of its existence:

> We affirm the philosophical or religious ideal of non-violence as the foundation of our purpose, the presupposition of our faith, and the manner of our action. Non-violence as it grows from the Judaic-Christian traditions seeks a social order of justice permeated by love. Integration of human endeavor represents the first step towards such a society. . . .

Clearly, the emphasis of the organization, in its earliest days, was upon the tactic of non-violent, direct action as the only legitimate means of achieving justice in the American social order and not upon a precise and delimited definition of the goals of non-violence. However, as the sit-in tactic utilized by the students expanded beyond lunch counters into segregated public toilets, public accommodations, and other areas where racial injustice thrived, SNCC found it necessary to "firm up" its definitions of the goals it sought to realize. The necessity of this step was also brought about by increasingly more vitriolic attacks from racist whites and negroes. Ex-president Harry S. Truman, for instance, accused the students active in the sit-ins of being communist affiliated and guided. Several prominent negroes accused the students of only seeking publicity and attention. SNCC, in response to these charges, defined its goals, in essence, as the development of a community in which man could realize the full meaning of the self, which demands open and equal relationships with others. It was specifically stipulated by the SNCC hierarchy that such a condition of life could be brought about through the active enforcement of laws guaranteeing the civil rights of all citizens in the United States. It was through achieving changes in such laws and seeing to their proper enforcement that the basic guarantees of freedom, justice, and equality, as stipulated by the constitution, could be realized, or so SNCC members thought.

In line with its avowed advocacy of the natural brother-hood of man and its belief in the desirability of a fully integrated society, SNCC was receptive to and even requested both the financial and active support of whites. And many whites, from all walks of American life, responded. Some joined SNCC out of religious conviction; some joined as a result of intra-psychic pressures resulting from a sort of intellectually derived moralism. Some joined the movement in order to protest against the course of events not ostensibly related to the plights of Black people in America. And, inevitably, some joined out of guilt, one of the most compelling emotions known to man. So, arm in arm, singing "We Shall Overcome," Black and white together surged across the south, enduring the brutality and non-violently absorbing the assaults of hundreds of racists in their efforts to realize a better society for all Americans. Taking a page from Martin Luther King's book on the strategy and moral foundations of non-violent, direct action, these rebels with a cause sought to appeal to the conscience of the south. They sought to demonstrate, with their blood, the basic righteousness and justice of their cause. Even the terror and horror of murders and lynchings by southern law-enforcement officials and citizens could not turn them from their goals. For there was little doubt in their minds that ultimately their efforts would meet with victory, if they would just persevere and keep the faith. And press on and keep the faith they did. They even expanded their efforts, in 1961, into activities aimed at desegregating interstate passenger transportation throughout the south. But, a festering tension and dissatisfaction over the pace of the movement among its less patient, but no less committed, Black members became increasingly apparent. Changing long-entrenched attitudes and activities of people who have known but a single system of Black-white relationships all their lives was necessarily physically costly and time consuming. And the results of sacrifices endured, time expended, and brutality absorbed did not always manifest themselves in the form of tangible goals. Although some short-term attainments were certainly far reaching and significant, many young Blacks in particular regarded the ratio of cost to reward as negatively proportionate. As one distraught Black SNCC member remarked in 1963, "How many hot-dogs and cups of coffee will Black people have to be served at newly integrated lunch counters to balance out the price paid in blood and human lives to desegregate those lunch counters and restaurants. How many times will we have to use formerly whites-only toilets before the ledger is balanced to the extent that the blood spilled in order to gain use of those toilets is compensated for?" And there was also the gnawing awareness among many young Black activists that despite the achievements of the movement, the basic human status relationships between Blacks and whites had not changed. To the contrary, the basic inequality of Black-white relations had seemingly become even more entrenched in response to the sit-ins and demonstrations. But, there were still other more important reasons underlying the growing dissatisfactions with the immediate direction and pace of the movement. It was primarily these more deep-seated discrepancies between expected results and actual achievements which paved the way both for changes in the principles of the revolt and the estrangement of former white allies from the movement.

1960-1966: The costs and the rewards

Although the movement initiated by Black students continued to expand in both the breadth of its activities and the intensity of its attacks, dissatisfaction and disaffection among its rank-and-file Black participants likewise continued to spread. Since its inception, SNCC had guided the efforts of the movement into the more diverse areas—voter registration drives in Mississippi and the establishment of "freedom schools" in Georgia and Alabama. It had also extended its organizational base beyond its home office in Atlanta to include permanently staffed facilities in all the major cities of the United States—in New York, Los Angeles, Chicago, St. Louis, Boston, New Orleans, Louisville, and others. White sympathizers organized a companion organization called "Friends of SNCC," which served primarily to funnel financial aid to SNCC from predominantly white colleges and communities in the north. It was essentially the experience and sophistication gained by rank-and-file SNCC members and the organization's leaders in branching out and diversifying their attacks on racism and injustice and the imbalance in the cost-reward relationships which brought all the dissatisfactions to a head.

As we mentioned, results of the first six years of the Black student movement were often intangible, seldom immediate, and always costly. Primarily through the efforts of SNCC, public facilities were desegregated by young Black and white students throughout the south. Racist white law officials, business owners, and voter registration officials were confronted and frequently overcome on their own ground. The publicity accorded plights of Black people in the south and the dramatic effects of the students' activities contributed to forcing the federal government to enter the struggle in many instances, ostensibly on the side of the students and the Black masses. Federal marshals were often sent to centers of student activity to protect civil rights workers and those working to register disfranchised Black citizens. New and more forceful legislation was passed by the federal government supposedly aimed at insuring that the guarantees of the United States Constitution would be upheld where the rights of minority group people were concerned. Emerging primarily from the interest shown by the federal government in the lot of Black people in the south, there occurred at this point in the movement a revitalization of many Black youths' faith in the potential for reform inherent in the processes of litigation and corrective legislation.

From their victories—and to a large extent from their

defeats as well—young Black students also gained a new sense of racial pride, relevance, and sophistication. The almost religious experiences of having fought the battles and taken the risks heightened their idealism and their determination to fight on to ultimate victory. However, not all of the results of the struggle had been positive. And, for some Black students, not even the sweet taste of victory could diminish their suspicions that an evil greater than those that they had directly confronted in the south lay in wait for them—nationwide institutionalized racism, tolerated and sometimes fostered overtly and covertly by the United States government itself.

REDEFINITION
AND
REAPPRAISAL

Although middle-class Black students had recognized from the very inception of their revolt the character and force of southern racism, very few were aware that an equally virulent strain pervaded the north and had infected the federal government itself. For had it not been the federal government and the force of northern arms that had freed the slaves. Had it not been the "Great White Fathers" in Washington, D.C. who had been responsible for instituting most of the major civil rights legislation in the nation from the thirteenth, fourteenth, and fifteenth amendments through the school desegregation act of 1954 to the civil rights bill of 1964. Indeed, had it not been the Confederation government which had drawn up and implemented the original civil rights bill, the bill of rights, in the interest of all whites, poor and rich alike.

With the election of Stokely Carmichael to the chairmanship of SNCC in 1966, both SNCC and the Black student revolt took on new directions and proportions that marked a major turning point in the struggle. These new directions and proportions were to bring about almost total financial bankruptcy of SNCC and, for all practical purposes, its demise as a politically cohesive and effective force in the Black student movement. But to the extent that SNCC and its leadership identified and clarified the obstacles faced by Black people in their struggle for freedom and gave that struggle new momentum and direction, freedom, justice, and equality for Afro-Americans were brought one step closer to becoming realities.

Chapter 3

A redefinition of the problem

Through their experiences and observations in both the north and south Black students came to realize that the enemy was comprised of forces much more extensive, complex, and interdependent than they had at first realized.

In the south, Black students had witnessed the seeming lack of capacity or willingness of the federal government to intervene and protect the lives of civil rights workers. They had seen federal troops stand by with empty rifles and sheathed bayonets as Black school children were spat upon and stoned by racist white mobs, ostensibly because such troops were ordered to act only upon such occasions when local law-enforcement personnel had attempted to restore order and failed; And they witnessed time and time again the spectacle of murderers and lynchers being acquitted of their crimes by white racist kangaroo courts and juries as the federal government stood silently by and refused to act because of "a question of legal jurisdiction."

In the north Black students and SNCC workers encountered the same contradictions between what the supposed role of the federal government was and what that role in fact was turning out to be. Even after federal legislation was passed, supposedly to correct these very problems, Black students active in the north were shackled in their efforts as masses of Black people sat confined to dilapidated slum tenements and fell prey to rats, exploitative slum landlords, merchants, loan sharks, and racially discriminating real estate agents. And all the while, the federal government pleaded that it could not act until all local avenues of redress had been exhausted or that, under the "separation of powers" stipulation in the Constitution, the branch of the federal government responsible for enforcing the laws of the land could not act in this or that instance. They watched as the federal government rejected proposal after proposal authorizing sorely needed funds to alleviate unsanitary conditions and to institute public health programs in northern Black communities. They saw election districts gerrymandered by local city and county governments to maintain the strength of machine politics in such areas and to, in effect, disfranchise Blacks. They saw the federal government stand by as racist cops were acquitted and presented with meritorious service awards after shooting Black teenagers to death, again because there was a question of "legal jurisdiction" involved.

The Black students needed no other proof, but there was plenty available.

When the Black rebellions began washing over America's cities in 1965, the national government immediately sent federal troops into Black communities with orders to "shoot to kill any looter, sniper, or arsonist" in defense of the lives and property of white racists who had been exploiting and oppressing these Black communities for decades. These troops, aided by local gestapos, functioning as law-enforcement officials, often shot randomly into slum tenements and at passing cars "suspected" of concealing or transporting loot, incendiary weapons, or guns. Innocent Black children, Black women, and old folks were, upon occasion, wantonly murdered. And the federal government was adjudged directly guilty of and responsible for these acts by Black students, both north and south of the Mason-Dixon line.

The following excerpt from Sidney M. Willhelm's "Red Man, Black Man and White America: The Constitutional Approach to Genocide" (published in the *Catalyst*, Spring, 1969 issue) portrays one aspect of the perspective of young Blacks toward American society during the period of transition from a non-violent direct action, integrationist orientation to the Black Power phase of the movement. Mr. Willhelm utilizes a comparative approach toward anti-minority violence by white America.

The [Afro-American], in terms of racism, rises into white consciousness as but an impediment much as whites took the

Redefinition and reappraisal

Indian to be a disposable irritant in the relentless westward thrust to realize the nation's nineteenth-century manifest destiny. . . .[1] the racist virus dooms the [Blacks], just as the Indian, to dismissal; . . . White America now extends palliatives in the form of welfare measures, private enterprise employs the slum [Blacks] to reduce Black hostility from threatening economic losses in property that come with [Black] insurrections until such time as White America mobilizes sufficient military force to subdue the restless [Black] into a listless Negro. The initial white restraint will be interpreted by whites as a "genuine" expression of compassion rather than a tactic intended to stall off the Blacks until mobilization can be arranged. But after the period of "fairness" will come the reign of white terror upon the [Afro-American], . . .

The nation, with a strong commitment to a tradition of violence, resorts to a police state first to contain black-skinned people in isolation from white contact and, second to restrain any threat from breaking out of the reservation in the event of violence. Thus, the matter of police brutality becomes, at most, a secondary abuse for the oppressed ghetto Blacks; a police force assigned to preserve "law and order" remains fundamentally racist even in the total absence of brutality because it is charged with the responsibility to uphold the separation of all Americans according to race. . . . The enforcement of Constitutional Equality inevitably means the entrenchment of racism by the racial separation which comes in its wake. No amount of proper etiquette on the part of police, therefore, nullifies the basic racist machinery which results from imposing "law and order" according to Constitutional Equality. The law, itself, comes into doubt among [Blacks] with or without police brutality accompanying enforcement.

The discretion by a White America to resort to extermination for restoring "law and order" over a rebellious Black community receives ample confirmation. Of the 34 deaths officially certified by the McCone investigation of the Watts insurrection, only 3 were whites; the *Detroit Free Press* established 43 killings during the Detroit upheaval and insisted "the Guard was involved in a

[1]Fritz, *op cit.*, p. 114.

total of eleven deaths in which nine innocent people died"; of the 26 persons killed in Newark, only 3 were whites.* During and after each incident, official statements and news reports carried the message of Blacks attacking whites when, in fact, the reverse would be a more accurate account of what transpired. . . .

While thousands of Blacks were arrested for a variety of charges and hundreds found guilty and punished, not one guardsman has been charged and brought to trial in complete disregard for the testimony by the commanding officer. Indeed, the militia received virtually unqualified praise such as from Governor Hughes of New Jersey during the Newark outbreak who was "thrilled" by the exemplary behavior. . . . Such white response typifies the reaction to wrongs committed against the American Indian: relatively few whites were ever brought to justice for crimes as extreme as murder committed against the Indian; even fewer found guilty; and most sentences meted out were slight punishments amounting, in effect, to perfunctory administration of "justice." . . .

America Is A Nation Of White People Marking Time For A Black People (emphasis mine.) After three centuries of abuse, the white majority repudiates the Black minority for the very qualities for which it must accept blame: poverty, ignorance, family disruption, filth, crime, disease, substandard housing. While assuring majestic prospects for acceptance, the nation removed the basic opportunities for achievement; now that Blacks burst forth with insurrection, whites exploit the protest to reciprocate with more massive violence until full suppression befalls the resisting Afro-Americans. The white strategy reflects the nation's earlier history when "the ingenious plan evolved of first maddening the Indians into war, and then falling upon them with exterminating punishment," all along branding the latter with the charge of aggression.

Indignity, oppression, injustice, unconcern, these are the

*The figures vary from one account to another, but the extremely small number of white deaths remains constant despite the variance. The facts presented here reflect the shifting estimates.

words that mark the sordid story. In 1966, during the tenure of a Democratic-controlled congress and a Democratic presi-dent who was committed to the realization of the "Great Society" for all Americans, it took a major effort to gain appropriations for aiding poverty-stricken Black communities, admittedly insufficient funds at that. During the tenure of that same congress and that same president, there was only token executive and congressional resistance to the appropriation of hundreds of billions of dollars to finance space exploration, to increase still further the more than sufficient supply of terror weapons in America's offensive and defensive arsenal, and to subsidize private big business and industry. In 1969, some members of congress threatened to cut space appropriations if U.S. astronauts put any but an American flag on the moon. Yet that same congress had been unable to find any fat in the space budget when Black spokesmen suggested in February of that year that the space program be cut in order to free more funds for rural and urban slum rehabilitation. Small wonder that many Blacks began having second thoughts about their unbroken support of Democratic candidates since the time of Franklin D. Roosevelt.

The government's international record was equally dismal. American troops were sent into the Dominican Republic to shore up the faltering, white-dominated, oppressive regime in that country, and in the process, killed or wounded scores of Dominican citizens. But there was no "legal question of jurisdiction" involved here—at least none that the United States government recognized.

In southeast Asia, the executive branch of the federal government had committed several hundred thousand United States troops and untold billions in war materials to wars now raging in Laos, Thailand, Viet Nam, and Cambodia while incendiary fires ate at the nation's capital, and pockets of poverty and hunger made a mockery of the American dream. Where was the government's concern for legal questions of jurisdiction when it embarked upon these acts of international genocide and criminality, acts which the entire world condemned as illegal, immoral, and unethical? It was essentially contradictions in policy and practice such as these which led SNCC and its Black student members to a redefinition of the problems faced by Black people.

Conceptually, the problem was redefined as institutionalized racism. Its essential elements were overt and covert cooperation between local, state, and national governments to deprive and deny Black people of their constitutional and human rights; the conscious and unconscious acts of business enterprises and private white and negro citizens that prevent Black people from gaining such rights; and the inherently racist and anti-Black character of this society's social, economic, political, educational, and religious institutions.

It was SNCC, this time under the tutelage of its new chairman, Stokely Carmichael, which led the way in reorienting Black students to this redefinition of the problem. In carrying out its task, the SNCC hierarchy saw as its chief responsibility the need to redefine the situation and position of Black people in American society. Blacks had to begin to perceive themselves not as free citizens but as colonized vassals under the heel of an oppressive and heartless system that seemed bent on carrying out a systematic and deliberate campaign of racist injustice to its inevitable conclusion—Black genocide. SNCC sought to bring about a new consciousness among Black people which would enable them to proceed effectively against institutionalized racism. In Carmichael's words:

This consciousness might be called a sense of peoplehood, pride rather than shame in Blackness, and an attitude of brotherly, communal responsibility among all Black people for one another. In short, if I had to sum up this consciousness, I would define it as the undying love of Black people for Black people. A willingness not only to suffer and die for the oppressed Black masses, but a willingness to kill for them if necessary.

In a nutshell then, in light of the new definition of the problem, SNCC sought to encourage a new consciousness among Black people; to develop and suggest new and politically relevant means of expressing that consciousness; and to provide leadership, as a vanguard group, in devising new tactics in order to achieve freedom, justice, and equality for the Black masses.

It was obvious to the SNCC leadership, as it was to many in the rank and file, that in a situation where almost every facet of a social order has a vested interest in maintaining a racist, oppressive, and anti-Black status quo, appeal to conscience was almost certainly going to be largely ineffectual as a tactic for bringing about change, and, at best, it would result in inconsequential concessions achieved at a monotonously slow and costly pace. Clearly, a reappraisal of tactics was due.

A reappraisal of tactics and means

Guided by the redefined problem, the SNCC hierarchy arrived at a decision, reached long before by many people in the Black communities of America, that, strategically, the tactic of non-violent, direct action, when employed as an almost dogmatic, religious exercise, was too shackling to allow Blacks to move effectively against their enemy. The outcry from whites affiliated with SNCC, who had supported the organization morally and contributed financially to its activities, was immediate and decidedly against any shift away from the strategy of non-violence. It almost seemed as if whites were more concerned about maintaining the method than achieving the goals of the struggle. But under any circumstances, Black students had little choice but to approve and endorse the diversification of tactics.

Whites reacted immediately. Most dropped out of SNCC. For all practical purposes, the organizational affiliate of SNCC, which had been established by liberal whites to provide it with financial aid, the so-called Friends of SNCC, disappeared from the nation's predominantly white northern college campuses, which had served as that group's bases of operation. SNCC's operating annual budget—the bulk of which was financed by liberal northern whites—dropped from $250,000 in 1963 to almost nothing by the summer of 1966. Many whites felt betrayed. Those who had joined the organization out of religious duty and convictions felt now that it was against their religious principles to support or be active in an organization which, in effect, had proposed a philosophy bordering upon Black separatism and denounced as untenable a dogmatic adherence to the strategy of non-violence based upon the virtues of redemptive suffering. Those whites who had joined SNCC in order to swab their guilt-ridden consciences by "joining hands and working with Blacks" saw their essentially selfish hopes dashed. But for all practical purposes it was just as well that whites were deserting the cause. For in light of the new orientation of the Black movement, their future potential effectiveness within SNCC would have been minimal.

In line with its new emphasis on Black consciousness and Black unity, the SNCC hierarchy decided that three immediate changes in its organizational structure had to be made. First of all, as the vanguard organization in the Black student movement—if not the entire civil rights struggle— SNCC felt that Black people should man all the positions of authority and power in the organization at both the local and national levels. This was not an anti-white move, as many of those whites who had remained in SNCC assumed it to be. It was pro-Black. It was a move primarily aimed at making SNCC a more efficient organization and one aimed at accustoming Blacks to handling the reins of leadership and power in their own organization. It was partially true, however, as most Blacks alleged, that whites, no matter how liberal they are, never simply join predominantly Black organizations. They infiltrate them and take them over. Many times this has not been deliberate on the part of whites. Often they have simply had more experience in formal organization and therefore were more competent and capable in running such groups as SNCC. So almost naturally they rose to positions of leadership more readily than did their less experienced Black comrades. Even when whites are not physically involved in organizational activities, they traditionally have still been able to control the balance of power and authority in such organizations by manipulating the amount and distribution of the funds which they have contributed. Some of the remaining white SNCC members had a visceral reaction to SNCC's move to appoint Blacks to all positions of power and authority in the organization. Coming hard on the heels of the new strategy of diversifying SNCC tactics as proposed by the group's hierarchy, this was simply too much. So they picked up their marbles, and they, too, deserted the struggle. For many were unwilling merely to serve and give up the positions of power that they had held, even if the movement might ultimately benefit.

The second move made by SNCC was to officially advocate the notion that Blacks should be the only organizational representatives in direct contact with and · working within the Black communities of America. This advocacy was based upon the idea that Blacks were better able to understand the problems faced by oppressed Black people and that they were better able to communicate with the Black masses and thus to offer them aid and advice. More important, SNCC felt that Black people could accomplish these ends without demeaning other Blacks in need of help. Young Blacks, SNCC leaders believed, were less likely than whites to have ulterior motives for getting involved with the Black community, such as assuaging guilt feelings and religious hang ups and satisfying an exaggerated sense of moralism and righteousness. The chances were much better that Blacks would be motivated primarily to help other Blacks.

Underlying the emphasis on Black control of the movement was the obvious need for the Black masses to see and to feel that they were being led and helped by other Blacks. Black students have been aware for some time that if Black people, and young Black children in particular, see whites—regardless of their political persuasions—as being the prime movers in efforts to liberate Black people, then to the extent that those efforts succeed, those people grow to respect and revere whites, not Blacks. This is one of the major reasons why, until very recently, before the actual truth about him was made known to Afro-Americans, Black people respected Abraham Lincoln so intensely. After all, through his efforts their enslaved forebears had been freed. If Blacks assume leadership in the struggle, then to the extent that they are effective, the Black masses will grow to respect, love, and revere Blacks—and, in effect, themselves. Blacks identify naturally with other Blacks; very seldom, with white leadership figures.

In essence, then, SNCC's policy of making Blacks the primary liaison agents between the organization and the Black community of America was based upon one relatively simple and intuitively obvious notion: He who is granted his freedom by another man merely exchanges masters, but he who achieves his own freedom becomes his own master. The white liberal "backlash" reaction to this step: more white defections from SNCC, more accusations of "Black racism," and an even further drop in financial support.

The last step, taken by SNCC within the new format, was to make all its chapters primarily responsive to the needs and desires of the Black people in the local areas served. Under such a setup, no longer could anyone—negro or white—manipulate or control the organization down through and including local action programs either through financial contributions or positions of authority and power. What local people felt to be their problems and needs would be the determining factor in arriving at decisions as to what problems would be attacked at the local level. To the remaining white members of SNCC, this was the last straw. This final "affront," they felt, was a blatant act of ingratitude, a flagrant statement of mistrust, and a final manifestation of "Black racism." And thus another step was taken toward white estrangement from the Black student movement and toward the dissolution of the Black-liberal white alliances that had characterized the movement during its first six years.

But, as we mentioned, for all practical purposes it was just as well that most whites had deserted the ranks of SNCC voluntarily, because given the new definition of the problem and the new strategies devised for dealing with that problem, it was highly unlikely that they would have been able to function effectively within SNCC.

The foundations upon which this evaluation of the political effectiveness of white liberals rests were well grounded. In a society where racism and anti-Black sentiments are so strong, so institutionalized, and so much a part of the entire fabric of society, where even some Blacks have become anti-Black negroes, it is inconceivable that any white person, regardless of his political persuasions, should escape the effects of such poisoning. Although it is true, as Carmichael has stated, that all negroes are potentially Black people—and that most certainly some Black people are potential traitors to their race—it is equally true that all whites are anti-Black to some extent. Many are rabidly anti-Black. And a "little" racism is like a "little" strychnine—enough to put on the head of a pin is deadly. As such, from the point of view of the organization's leadership, it would have been ludicrous for SNCC to tolerate within its organizational structure any identifiable racists. The danger from negroes arises after the fact, because they can readily "pass" as Black people. Not so with whites. In a society reeking of racism, where the mass media, religion, the educational and political systems, communicate to whites the myth of their innate racial superiority over all other races of human beings, it would be foolhardy for Blacks, in particular, to assume that somehow

37

any white has remained free of racist contamination, no matter how sincere his offers of help. In partial recognition of this fact, in the latter half of 1966, SNCC formally excluded all whites from the organization.

There were other reasons for the exclusion. The SNCC leadership recognized that institutionalized racism relies upon the active support and dissemination of anti-Black attitudes and practices in the United States. In this country, an almost "instinctive" sense of white superiority prevails among whites. They pick up this warped and corrupt attitude wherever they turn—in school, at work, in taverns, social clubs, at their mother's knee, and in all manner of other joints. In fact, they absorb racism as a regular part of the American socialization process. Institutionalized racism in the United States operates to the advantage of all whites—except perhaps those who are too mentally incompetent, culturally deprived, insane, or just plain trifling to "benefit" from it. Although many "respectable" whites would never bomb a church and kill four Black girls, spit upon or stone a Black student or family, or unleash vicious dogs on unarmed and defenseless Black women, they do stand by—sometimes unaware, often unconcerned, and almost always silently—as the loathsome toll of racism—death, degradation, humiliation—piles up. It is the "respectable" whites, as well as southern crackers, who continue to support the racist institutions of this society. It is the "respectable" whites, as well as racist political officials, who continue to support or tolerate programs of increased military and industrial-subsidy expenditures while Black babies in Harlem, Mississippi, and South Carolina starve. And, it is the "respectable" whites, as well as the racists, who yearly occupy jury seats in the north and south and send Black people to the jails of this country for relatively petty offenses while organized crime preys on and destroys Black communities across the land. Small wonder that white liberal cries for civil rights in the south in 1964 turned to demands for law and order in the north in 1968. To the "respectable" white liberals, SNCC and its Black student members were saying in 1966, "White folks, this too is racism."

The negro constantly walks with the burden of racial oppression on his back, but unlike Blacks, he accommodates to it and cooperates with it. He simply does not have the guts or the desire to confront it. If given the opportunity, he voluntarily subscribes to anti-Black attitudes and practices in an effort to escape the realities of the Black experience in America and the hard, grinding task of changing that experience. Most Black people cannot escape the grim realities of life in racist white America. For those who could "turn negro" but do not, accommodation represents too great an affront to their human dignity, their inherent idealistic spirit, their racial pride, and their sense of identity. And in these respects they differ significantly from both negroes and whites.

In essence, then, SNCC, as the *avant-garde* organization of the Black student movement, undertook to redefine the racist problem in America and to reappraise traditional tactics upon coming to grips with one central fact—the revelation that insofar as whites are concerned there has never existed an "American Dilemma" in the United States. Whites of virtually all political, religious, and ethical persuasions have functioned in complicity with or tolerated institutionalized racism in this society. So compelling are the rewards to be gained by conforming and accommodating to racism and so complete is the degree to which American society is and has been permeated by this affliction, that a whole new breed of humanity has been created and perpetuated in the United States—the American negro.

As a result of the efforts of SNCC, the Black student movement advanced to another level of political awareness, sophistication, and relevance. The format that SNCC laid out for the organization and functioning of Black political groups was to become the blueprint for the Black student unions, which, in 1966, were already beginning to appear on the nation's college campuses and in its high schools. But the price SNCC paid for its radical departure from traditional tactics was high. Nevertheless, move radically and deliberately it did, and the entire Black student movement moved along with it.

NEW PROPHETS
AND
NEW DIRECTIVES

During the first six years of the Black student revolt, that period covering 1960-1966, the more traditional civil rights leaders had been the primary charismatic, philosophical, and inspirational figures in the movement. Such men as Bayard Rustin, James Farmer, Whitney Young, Roy Wilkins, and, of course, the late Rev. Dr. Martin Luther King, Jr., had more or less set the general context, by example, within which the student struggle would be waged. For these idealistic young Black students knew of no other contemporary frameworks or guidelines to follow in carrying out a struggle aimed at gaining freedom, justice, and equality for Afro-Americans. Within that six-year period, however, many students were catching up with and passing their mentors. Some of these historical giants would fall by the wayside. Some would become irrelevant. And others would find themselves trying to keep up with the student movement or following it rather than setting its pace and dictating its direction.

Most young Black students today do not even know who Bayard Rustin is. Here is a man who, for an amazingly long period of time, was the "philosopher" of the civil rights movement and actually helped to organize and plan the now legendary "March on Washington." But today, for Black students, his political and philosophical relevance is nil.

Right after the March on Washington, James Farmer dropped out of the movement completely as an active formulator and implementor of tactics. Up until that time, he had been the most articulate and brilliant leader ever to head the Congress of Racial Equality, which he had helped to found.

Chapter 4

He resigned in 1970.

Today, he occupies a secondary position in the bureaucracy of President Richard Nixon's cabinet and is regarded by Black students generally as part of the establishment.

Among Black students, both Whitney Young and Roy Wilkins have fallen from favor. Whitney Young, who has been tagged "Whitey" Young by the present generation of young Blacks, is considered a front man for liberal whites, who are neither aware of nor willing to move in the directions necessary to solve the problems of the masses of Black people. As director of what is perceived as a "bourgeois, middle-class, negro" oriented organization—the Urban League—"Whitey" Young, too, is seen as irrelevant.

Roy Wilkins, secretary of the National Association for the Advancement of Colored People, apparently has degenerated beyond mere irrelevancy. Some of his statements and acts have whipped up storms of criticism from Blacks, particularly his statement of March 10, 1969, to the effect that the N.A.A.C.P. would initiate legal action against any college or university conceding to Black student demands for separate housing facilities, separate dining facilities, and separate autonomous Black studies institutes and colleges. Numerous rumors of plots against his life have evoked satisfaction or remarks such as, "It's long overdue" among Black students on several of the nation's more active college campuses. For the present generation of Black people, he seems finished as a leader or spokesman, all his past contributions notwithstanding.

The late Dr. Martin Luther King was widely loved and respected by all those involved in the Black liberation struggle. The sole criticism directed against him by many Black students was that his religious dedication rendered him too inflexible to meet effectively the challenges and problems of racism and injustice in their more complex and wider context. Dr. King most certainly agreed with the young Blacks' appraisal that institutionalized racism was the overriding problem. But he differed with them on many of their proposed solutions to the problem. For Dr. King was a preacher and a man whose feet traveled in the same direction as his words. If he had embraced the practice of expelling whites from Black political organizations or if he had openly advocated the use of "any means necessary" to solve the problems faced by Black people, he would have had to leave the pulpit. Such was the nature of his honesty, integrity, and sincerity of purpose. But he chose to remain a preacher. He also chose to continue his advocacy of non-violent direct action as the only legitimate means of achieving true freedom, justice, and equality. In doing so, however, he found himself trying to keep pace with the Black student revolt rather than guiding it. But the bulk of the young Afro-Americans in the student movement never lost faith in Martin Luther King as an inspirational figure and a Black man. Today they seek to keep his memory alive by having scholarship programs, dormitories, academic departments, and college recreational facilities named after him.

These traditional spokesmen and leaders did not, however, lose favor with Black students solely as a result of their own inflexibilities and imperceptiveness. Perhaps the main reason for their diminished prestige was the emergence of new "prophets," who addressed themselves more directly to the new orientations, hopes, idealism, and hunger for more aggressive action manifested by Black students during the mid-sixties. Many articulate and forceful young new voices emerged to fill the gaps created by the waning popularity and appeal of the men we have just discussed. Huey Newton, Minister of Defense for the Oakland, California, based Black Panther Party; Ron Karenga, the cultural nationalistic leader of the Los Angeles based "US" organization; and Charles Kenyatta, the head of New York City's Mau Mau's — all commanded significant respect among young Blacks in various local areas where these organizations had set up offices. But the three men who not only captured the attention of most

43

Black students but also their minds, were Malcolm X, Stokely Carmichael, and H. Rap Brown. These men reflected the spirit of the times, and their messages to young Blacks were unmistakable.

St. Malcolm X

Between 1960 and 1966, an entire generation of Black students had passed in and out of America's negro and predominantly white colleges and universities, and a new generation was half-way through its college career. By the end of this period, some of the original participants in the Black student revolt had graduated from school and taken jobs or gotten married. Others had been drafted into the armed forces, unwittingly helping to perpetuate genocide against the Vietnamese people. Still other Black students remained on the college campuses of the nation, but, for various reasons such as the pressures of marriage and raising a family, which necessitated the taking on of a part-time or full-time job as well as full-time school attendance, they ceased to be active participants in the struggle. But other older warriors, who had also remained, were still active and still determined. Younger Black college students, some of whom were new to the revolt or fresh from insulated middle-class negro backgrounds, soon caught the spirit of the new phase of the struggle. The man who most inspired them and articulated their aspirations was Malcolm X. By 1966, Malcolm X had already been dead for a year, the victim of assassins' bullets in New York City. But a testimony to his brilliance and forcefulness is the fact that even from the grave he managed to incite and excite a whole generation of young Afro-Americans, who had already begun to question both the motives and sincerity of anyone "over thirty." Malcolm, at the time of his death, was thirty-nine.

Some Black students first became acquainted with the ideas of Malcolm X through his autobiography and a book of

44

his speeches called *Malcolm Speaks*, which was, as was his autobiography, published posthumously. But most Black students came to know him as a powerful orator, *avant-garde* figure in the Black liberation struggle, and as "Our Black and Shining Prince" via the medium of long-playing record albums, which were sold in most of the "soul" music shops across the country. It was, then, the man himself who spoke to these young Afro-Americans and, in line with the new spirit of their struggle, they listened, absorbed, and savored his every word—then they listened again. Books, articles, magazines, pamphlets, record albums, and tapes by and about Malcolm X became treasured items, particularly the record albums "Message to the Grassroots" and "Ballots or Bullets." Many of these young Afro-Americans had never even been aware of Malcolm X while he was alive.

Malcolm X's appeal to young Black students stems from a number of factors. First of all, he was undeniably and unalterably not merely in Black America—he was of it. Malcolm was its native son. He had left a Black community in the Mid-west and become "Big Red"—a pimp, hustler, dope pusher, and thief in New York's Harlem in the 1940's. Unlike most of the traditional spokesmen in the struggle—and most of the students themselves—Malcolm was not and had never been in the middle-class negro "bag." He knew the oppressed Black masses; he knew the "streets;" he knew, from firsthand experience, what made the Black masses laugh, what made them cry, and what made them fight. For more so than any Black freedom fighter since Nat Turner, Malcolm X was truly of the people—he belonged to them. He had shared their miseries, their joys, and their hopes. Malcolm X fitted ideally into the new context of the Black student revolt. He was right on time.

Malcolm's appeal to Black students was heightened by the direct and straightforward manner in which he articulated the problems faced by Black people and proposed solutions to them. Over and over again, using simple imagery and analogies, Malcolm X drove home the truth about the position of Black people in America. No institution, organization, or individual was too sacred or too high for Malcolm to attack and expose—presidents, the christian church, even some "civil rights" organizations if he adjudged them guilty of oppressing Afro-Americans and people of color all over the world or ignoring their plight. Today, Malcolm's most unguarded utterances constitute passwords in the Black student revolt.

The man was audacious. He evinced an iconoclastic fervor, which matched the rebellious nature of the students themselves. At a time when many whites had deserted the movement completely over the question of tactics, and many traditional civil rights spokesmen had chosen, indirectly, to become irrelevant as leaders rather than abandon the strategy of non-violent, direct action or expel whites from within the ranks of their organizations, Malcolm was openly and flagrantly advocating "Black liberation—by any means necessary." And although he did not popularize the concept, Malcolm had recognized and outlined as early as 1963 the character and nature of institutionalized racism in the language of the masses and also had proposed that Blacks alone should control and staff Black political organizations. It was not until 1966 that the Black student movement caught up with the brilliance and foresight of this man, who possessed not a single academic credential, not even a high school diploma.

Whites feared Malcolm, when he was alive and after he was dead. This was a new phenomenon in the movement. Whites had patronized Black people, some had pitied them, and many had hated them, but except for ante-bellum southerners, few had feared them. Why fear a leaderless and despised rabble? But to white America, particularly during the last year of his life, Malcolm X was an irresponsible hate-monger, bent on destroying them and their society. He would not go away. Even after his death his mystical appeal to

Black Americans plagued and worried them. Young Black students "dug" the fact that Malcolm had managed, from the grave, to confuse, befuddle, and strike fear into the hearts of white folks—and negroes, too—while other spokesmen in the struggle were still concerned about alienating or otherwise getting white people angry or upset.

What finally and irrevocably linked Malcolm X with the Black students in America were the fact and circumstances of his death. He realized that he was marked for death yet he never wavered in the struggle, never permitted his idealism and sense of commitment to be diluted. He could have fled the country or gone into hiding. But he stayed, and he functioned, and he died—many Blacks felt for them.

The circumstances surrounding Malcolm's death were in and of themselves significant. There have been many theories proposed to explain Malcolm's death, but there is little question in the minds of most young Black students concerning who is really responsible for his death—the United States Central Intelligence Agency. They believe that Malcolm had become too powerful, domestically and internationally, for the U.S. government to tolerate him politically. His open advocacy of the establishment of international ties between Afro-Americans and the Moslem (or Muslim) and Black nations of Africa, and his efforts toward these ends are regarded by Black students as the real reasons behind his assassination. They do not hold the negroes, who actually pulled the triggers, any more responsible for Malcolm's death than they do the weapons themselves. For both the gunmen and the guns were only the tools. The real brains and the real criminals behind the murder, or so the students feel, are perched in high places in the bureaucracy of the United States government.

This conception of how and why Malcolm died fits neatly into the students' belief that the U.S. government has been as much responsible for Black oppression as the most rabid racists themselves. To them, Malcolm X had sought out the enemy, exposed him, sought to confront him, but had been diabolically and treacherously assassinated before he could neutralize him. But the fact that he had expected to die before he achieved his goals and yet had continued to press the confrontation made him a martyr and a saint in the minds and hearts of Black students in America.

Malcolm X's message to Black students was clear, concise, and unmistakably explicit. In essence, his directives were, first, that Black people must control their own communities and the resources and institutions of those communities; second, that Black people must not hesitate to use whatever means necessary to accomplish those goals; third, that Black people must develop an ethic—and he proposed Black Nationalism—that would unify them and prevent any outside group from ever again taking control of Black movements and communities; and, fourth, that Black people must recognize that their primary enemy was, is, and has always been the legally established institutions and government of the United States of America and anyone—negro or white—who supports those institutions or that government in its efforts to maintain the status quo.

To Black students, these directives meant a number of things. They meant, first of all, that Black people should forget about "integrating" white neighborhoods, restaurants, and schools and move to control their communities themselves. Malcolm was extremely convincing when he told Blacks to "turn inward" and emphasized the necessity of "Black control of Black communities" even before they thought about "turning outward" and integrating with whites. In Malcolm's way of thinking, the masses of Black people would always live in predominantly Black communities—just as most whites would always live in predominantly white communities. Thus it seemed ridiculous and absurd to him to base the liberation struggle on the notion that somehow, Blacks from all levels and strata in Black society would eventually move into white communities. What of the Black communities? Would whites move into an empty Harlem, or Watts, or the Fillmore District and subject their children to rats, roaches, and firetraps simply for the sake of perpetuating integration? No, not likely. Those who moved from the Black community to white areas almost certainly would be—as has always been the case—bourgeois middle-class negroes who have been the chief "house pets" of whites for generations. The masses would still live in grinding poverty and oppression. So, this being the case, it seemed self-defeating, to Malcolm, for the leaders of the struggle to expose the masses of Black people—including Black women and children—to the brutality and criminality of racist white mobs and police in order to open up integrated communities in which most of them would never be able to live anyway. And, even when white communities had been "integrated," it usually was not long before, as Malcolm stated—". . . all the whites left, and, there were the Blacks—all alone and by themselves again." Malcolm's mandate to young Black students was clear—to forget about busing, marching, and sitting-in and return to the Black communities of America and build those communities up to the point where crackers would feel compelled to petition the United States government for legislation that would protect their rights to move into Harlem, Watts, and other Black communities where Blacks had built good housing and good schools and enjoyed the good life.

Another of Malcolm's directives, which was picked up by Black students, was his notion that all authorities not appointed, controlled, or elected by the Black masses should be ejected—by force, if necessary—from all Black communities. For Blacks to tolerate or support the existence, within their communities, of authority figures whom they did not control, Malcolm felt, was the height of folly. This was particularly true in regard to people who functioned in Black communities as representatives of the law. In Malcolm's mind, it was no accident that white communities are protected by white cops and that in almost all cases white judges preside over criminal court cases arising within those communities. Whites would blow the switchboards at police stations in their communities to protest if white housewives woke up one morning to find that negro cops were patrolling their neighborhoods. But Black people not only see white cops—or a white cop and a negro companion—armed and patrolling their communities, but also see them brutalizing and murdering Black men, women, and children.

To Malcolm it seemed reasonable that if people who lived in Black communities controlled the police forces in those communities, then brutality and legalized murder of Blacks would not occur. Blacks would not tolerate the election, or appointment, or hiring of white cops and judges or the hiring of negro cops—none of whom resided in the Black community. If a cop lived in the Black community, he would be less likely to brutalize and murder Black people, because these people would be his neighbors and he would have to answer to them for his behavior. He would also be less likely to submit to pay-offs or otherwise allow crime to flourish unchecked in the Black community, because his wife, his daughters, and his kin would have to live in that community. In this regard, it is no coincidence that when white cops get word that a dope pusher, rapist, murderer, gangster, or prostitute is operating in or has even passed through a white community, they respond as if a major crime wave had broken out. Their families live there. What more incentive does any man need to seek to uphold justice and protect a community?

A similar line of argument underlay Malcolm's advocacy of Black control of the judiciary in their communities especially in the area of criminal adjudication. No judge or juror who has not lived under the same political or social pressures as Black people can render a just decision in trials where Blacks are facing criminal charges. All too often, the judge and the jurors themselves are directly responsible for bringing about, perpetuating, or supporting the very circumstances that most times force Black people to move illegally to satisfy

50

their needs and desires in this racist society. So we have Blacks in the position of being judged by Black oppressors! Whites are not qualified morally, ethically, or in any other way to judge in any fashion whatsoever the behavior or acts of Black people. And negroes are even less competent to do so than whites. For they deliberately seek first to satisfy white interests, regardless of whether justice is served or not.

This being the case, then, Malcolm saw the necessity of Blacks taking over the law-enforcement and judiciary processes of their communities. And he also saw that, since white control and white domination of these institutions was a functional necessity in racist white America, this could not be done easily. Whites would not relinquish control of Black communities without a fight. And this fight, quite possibly, would be violent. But this prospect, in Malcolm's words, ". . . should not deter Blacks from doing whatever is necessary to take over (these institutions). . . . Not to do so is to subject Black women, Black children, and Black men to wanton, arbitrary, and legal murder at the hands of whites and negroes." For Black students, a continuation of this trend was to be precluded at all costs.

A third directive issued by Malcolm X and adopted by Black students as a plank in their new program for Black liberation had to do with the development and deliberate perpetuation of an active identification with the new Black nations of Africa. Malcolm recognized that all movements utilizing "peoplehood" or nationalism as a means of achieving liberation had land as their basis. This involved not merely the physical acquisition of land upon which a people could establish a new nation, but also, and more important, it encompassed a psychological identification by that people with some definable land mass. Malcolm knew how committed American Jews were to the support of Israel, even though most never intend to live there. He recognized, too, the contradictory and racist character of criticisms leveled by whites and negroes at Black people who referred to themselves as

Afro-Americans and who showed an interest in and concern about Black African nations. Although whites and negroes have charged that it is ridiculous for Blacks to identify with Black Africa because most of them know nothing about the geography, languages, or Black people of that continent, they see nothing inconsistent about whites who refer to themselves as French-Americans or Russian-Americans or German-Americans, even though most know nothing about France, Russia, or Germany. They see nothing absurd about whites of Irish descent celebrating St. Patrick's Day, even though most know nothing about Ireland. Even negroes wear green on St. Pat's Day, and obviously they are not of Irish descent. But, Malcolm recognized—as do whites—that it is necessary for people to identify with an existence beyond the immediate past. He grasped how important it was for Blacks to perceive of themselves as having had a glorious and long history prior to their enslavement by the whites of Europe and America; that they understood that they did not simply spring from the soil in 1619, along with the cotton they chopped, simply because the whites needed cotton choppers. So, for Malcolm, an identification with Africa was imperative. His concern was not so much with the notion that Blacks should seek immediately to control land beyond their local communities, but rather that they identify with the continent from which their forebears had been uprooted by whites.

Malcolm also realized that the interests of Black Americans and of Black Africans were inextricably entwined, and he sought to foster closer relations between all Black peoples everywhere. But his efforts were cut short by his untimely death. Stokely Carmichael took up the politicizing of Black people at precisely this point, however, and a second new "prophet" was born.

To young Black students, Malcolm X never really died. He is the eternal spiritual symbol of the present phase of the Black student revolt. He showed Black people the contradictions and shortcomings implicit in attempting to use non-violence as the sole strategy in their liberation efforts in a basically violent society; in seeking to integrate white communities in America; and in not focusing on the development and control of their own communities. Thus, young Black students learned from Malcolm's wisdom and were inspired by his courage. But, most important of all, many were moved to action, action not always conforming strictly to his teachings but influenced by them nonetheless. This is the truest test of the faith of any people in a leader, living or dead.

Stokely Carmichael

If any one figure in the entire Black liberation struggle can be termed "the living personification" of the Black student revolt, that person is Stokely Carmichael. He manifests its spirit, its vigor, its courage, its idealism, its determination —and its shortcomings. Himself a Howard University graduate and the product of a middle-class family, Stokely Carmichael had been active in the freedom struggle for over a decade by the time he assumed the chairmanship of SNCC in 1966. He had been spat upon, stoned, brutalized, battered by fire hoses, and jailed as a result of his efforts in the struggle. But through all these experiences he had matured and become one of the most apt and articulate spokesmen for the Black liberation struggle. Television newscasters, such as CBS's Mike Wallace, concede that Carmichael made greater use of the white-owned and controlled mass media as a tool of the Black freedom struggle than any other person in history—regardless of his race, his crusade, or the issues involved. To Black students, it seemed almost natural to turn to Carmichael for guidance after Malcolm was removed from the scene.

Carmichael, like Malcolm X, saw that the central problem facing Afro-Americans was not a lack of love for their country; not an "American Dilemma"; not that Black people were unprepared for full citizenship and rights; not a problem of individual racists, red-necks, honkies, and crackers. The overwhelming problem, as Carmichael saw it, and as Malcolm had seen it, was institutionalized racism. If institutionalized racism could be eradicated, individual racists could be dealt with easily and effectively by established judicial forces in the society.

Carmichael's answer was not an appeal to the consciences of whites; not the appointment or election of a few negroes to relatively high government positions; not a handful of token negroes living in predominantly white neighborhoods, or attending predominantly white schools or churches. His answer to institutionalized racism—Black Power!

It was in the Summer of 1966, during the so-called "Freedom March" through Mississippi—which had been started by James Meridith shortly before he was ambushed and wounded by a Mississippi cracker—that Carmichael first expounded upon this new and radical solution to the problem. The crucial components of Black Power were essentially the same factors that Malcolm X had elaborated time and time again. Black Power meant the total control of every Black community in America by the Black people who lived in them. It meant that Black people should control and decide their own social, economic, and political destinies. Black Power became the password of the Meridith freedom march. Young Blacks picked it up immediately. For them it verbalized the passionate protest and determination raging within them, feelings that no longer could be satisfied by holding hands with whites and singing "We Shall Overcome."

The more traditionally oriented leaders who joined in the march, such as Martin Luther King and Floyd McKissick, initially were cool to the concept, even though both eventually propagated their own version of it. King was chiefly concerned about the advocacy of separatism, which could be inferred from a call for *Black* power. He was also worried about the possibility that some would interpret such a forceful use of the word *Power* as a clear abandonment of non-violence as a strategy for achieving Black liberation. And not the least of his concerns was the potentiality of "white backlash" in response to any call for Black Power, because, or so Dr. King felt, the term was neither clearly nor easily definable. At the time McKissick agreed basically with Dr. King's assessment of Black Power, even though he eventually became one of its chief advocates. As a matter of fact, he became such a rabid supporter of the new "politics of liberation" that he was often accused of "out stoking Stokely" in his enthusiasm for the term.

From the very beginning, young Blacks, and Black students in particular, heeded the call for Black Power and its appeal to Black separatism. Blacks were already differentiated from whites in America. If they were not, then there would be no Watts, no Roxbury, no Harlem. The implicit and explicit message of force, militancy, and aggressiveness inherent in the concept of *Power*, was, they felt, not only necessary, but desirable. And, what of King's concern for the so-called "white backlash?" The young Blacks felt in 1966, as they feel today, that Black people had been catching so much hell from the frontlash, that a backlash was really irrelevant. So Black Power soon became the password of the Black student revolt. And the symbol of Black Power—the raised, clenched fist—became as common on America's college campuses as libraries, text books, and marijuana.

Carmichael traveled to all parts of the United States, disseminating and explaining the new concept. He was particularly successful on college campuses. Black students understood and identified with it almost instinctively—just as white people, in general, were confused, frightened, or otherwise intimidated by its mere mention.

After the appeal and relevance of the phrase became evident, everyone began jumping on the bandwagon. And, each person defined the concept to fit his own bag. To jacklegged, tin-horned politicians, both negro and white, it meant the ability of Black people to vote or to serve as officers or delegates to the national convention of one or the other of the two major political parties. Therefore, when the negro Ralph Metcalf was permitted to help bring about the nomination of Hubert Humphrey for president of the United States on the Democratic ticket, this became an exercise in Black Power. Pseudo-capitalist negroes defined Black Power as "green power." Thus, when a negro sets up a store in a Black community and sells goods to Black people at exactly the same prices, or at higher prices, than white entrepreneurs charge, it becomes an exercise in Black Power. But as soon as that negro manages to steal enough money from the masses, he moves from the Black community, pays three or four times as much for a house as it is worth, and moves to some lily-white suburb. Yet in the mind of the pseudo-capitalist negro ("pseudo" because the system is so rigged that he will never be successful enough to be a real capitalist) this is Black Power. But students recognized the fallacies inherent in these and other opportunistic conceptualizations of Black Power. And one of the main figures who helped expose these fallacies was H. Rap Brown, Stokely Carmichael's successor as chairman of SNCC in 1967.

H. Rap Brown

Rap Brown is, perhaps, the Blackest man I have ever met. He is about six feet, five inches tall and of a smooth tan complexion. He is very intelligent, alert, and extremely articulate. Even more important, what most attracted Black students to Brown, was his audacity—his guts.

Rap, more so than either Malcolm X or Stokely Carmichael, addressed himself directly to the tasks and issues facing Black students. In his book, *Die, Nigger, Die*, he recorded an excellent synopsis of his message to Black students:

Negro college students have always felt themselves to be better than the brother on the block. Naturally, the brother would resent this and the first chance he got, he was upside the college student's head. That situation can only be overcome by the college student taking the initiative in overcoming whatever split might exist between himself and the blood on the corner. College students, however, get caught in a trick, because they think that to be accepted by the young bloods, they have to be tough, be a warrior. But all they have to do is show the brother that they respect him and that they recognize that he is a brother. All Black people are involved in the same struggle. Revolutionaries are not necessarily born poor or in the ghetto. There is a role for every person in the revolution if he is revolutionary. You don't have to throw a Molotov cocktail to be a revolutionary, right now, that is. One thing which the Black college student can do, at this time, is to begin to legitimatize the brother's actions—begin to articulate his position, because the college student has the skills that the blood doesn't have. It reminds me of the old story about the father and his son. The son comes to the father and says, "You told me that the lion was the king of the jungle. Yet in every story I read, the man always beats the lion. Why is that?" The father looks at the son and says, "Son, the story will always end the same until the lion learns how to write." If you don't begin to tell your own story, you will always be Aunt Jemima; you will always be "rioting." You must begin to articulate a position of your own.

The Black college student, if he is revolutionary, can help Black people to purge themselves of the misinformation that they've been fed all their lives. White nationalism has been instilled into us whether we know it or not. We have been told that George Washington should be our hero. George Washington is no hero of Blacks. He had 13 children and none by Martha. They were slaves! They tell us we should celebrate Christopher Columbus' birthday. Christopher Columbus was a 15th-century Eisenhower. He was trying to get to India. Did you ever see where India is on the map? But america has the power to legitimatize these people and make them heroes in our minds. America has negroes in the dilemma of thinking that everything Black is bad. Black cows don't give good milk; black hens don't lay eggs; black mail is bad; you wear black to funerals, white to weddings; angel food cake is white, devil's food cake is black. And all good guys wear white hats. And Black people fall for it. Everything Black is bad. That's white nationalism. And they tell you, you can't even talk about Black nationalism. So how do you combat it if you grow up telling your children that they should respect Santa Claus come December 25th when Santa is so white that he stays white even after he slides down a black chimney. But you tell your children that Santa Claus brought those toys and you take them to see a white Santa Claus. So therefore, it becomes instilled in their minds that Santa Claus is good because Santa Claus is white. Thus, we help foster that type of white nationalism. You must begin to define for yourself; you must begin to define your Black heritage. You must begin to investigate and learn on your own. They will never tell you that Hannibal was Black. They'll never tell you that African societies back in the 16th-century were the most modern known at that time and that the highest degree of culture existed there. Every time you open a book here in america, they gonna show you Uncle Tom's cabin or they gonna show you Double-O Soul with a piece of watermelon. It becomes the responsibility of the Black college student to combat this sort of thing. The education that a Black college student gets will be irrelevant, fruitless and worthless unless he uses it to define and articulate positions that are relevant to Black people. It does you no good to come to school and pledge to cross the burning sand. Hell, you ain't never got off the burning sand! Pledging is no good for Black people in america. When the man moves against you, your Omega sticker does not mean that he is going to pass you by. All it means is that he might take you to a different concentration camp. If you must pledge, pledge to be a revolutionary. You are involved in the struggle whether you want to be or not. Your badge of involvement is your skin. Therefore, you got to quit walking around talking about those people out there acting crazy. Them!! That's you!! Anything that we do will have a profound effect on you.

These men, then, are the three prophets whose ideas and

wisdom lie at the base of the present phase of the Black student revolt. The price of their contributions were high, both for themselves personally and for the struggle. These men, and others less well known but no less committed, have fallen before assassins, been placed under "house arrest," jailed, or hounded into exile in most cases by the U.S. government and its goon squad—the F.B.I. Malcolm X was shot down by order of persons unknown; Stokely Carmichael has left the country after harassment of both him and his wife, Miriam Makeba, reached intolerable levels; Rap Brown has been placed under house arrest by the U.S. government for "crimes" which have, as of yet, been neither clearly defined nor charged. Rap damn near has to have a visa to go to the toilet. Eldridge Cleaver was driven out of the country by the F.B.I., who have put out a warrant for his arrest based primarily on an act of self-defense committed while Cleaver was under attack by the Oakland, California, gestapo. Huey P. Newton is in jail, and neither the crime for which he was "tried" nor the basis for his fifteen-year sentence have been satisfactorily explained. Even Dr. King, sincere apostle of brotherhood and non-violence, was himself been shot down and killed by white *assassins*, only one of whom has been sent to jail. And it seems as if the U.S. government is doing all it possibly can not to bring to justice the people who conspired with James E. Ray to kill King, even though Ray, himself, admits that there was indeed a conspiracy. The recent ruling that Ray cannot be re-tried seems to have precluded the possibility of uncovering other conspirators. Even more ludicrous is the fact that the U.S. congress has entrusted the task of investigating the possibility of a conspiracy to James O. Eastland—supreme racist in this racist land. Perhaps Ray, too, will fall victim to "instant terminal cancer," as did Jack Ruby; or perhaps he will conveniently die some other way, as did the fifty-six people who might have shed some additional light on the J. F. Kennedy assassination. (It has been estimated that the chances of the fifty-six potential witnesses connected with the Kennedy asassination investigation all dying within a five-year period are approximately 300,000 trillion to one!)

But, Malcolm X, Huey Newton, Eldridge Cleaver, Rap Brown, Stokely Carmichael, and, most certainly, Dr. King, all realized that as individuals they were unimportant, that only peoples and ideals survive. And it was this realization that led them to continue their efforts even though they recognized the almost certain consequences of their actions. To their way of thinking, no man has a right to consider his individual well-being when the survival of his race and his people are at stake.

THE RETURN TO
THE CAMPUS

In 1967 and 1968, it became clear that Black Power had gripped the imaginations of Black students across America. It was equally obvious that the days had passed when Black students would leave the campus to sit-in at some segregated facility or another. Over 90% of the sit-ins initiated and implemented by Black students during this two-year period occurred on college campuses and not in segregated facilities in the society at large. And most of these sit-ins were not staged to protest against segregated conditions, but rather in order to pry compliance with Black student demands from white or negro administrators of colleges and universities. Most of these sit-ins, primarily on predominantly white campuses but at negro colleges as well, were designed to satisfy demands that were decidedly separatist in nature.

On the predominantly white college campuses, Black students saw change as necessary if such schools were to provide them with the preparation they needed to carry on as active participants in the Black liberation struggle within its new context. To this end, many individuals who had endured the defeats and victories of the integrationist-oriented phase of the student movement set about establishing Black student "unions" on predominantly white campuses. Regardless of what they have been called—The Association of Black Collegians, The Afro-American Society, The Black Students' Union, United Black Students, and so on—all are geared to provide Black students with a solid, legitimate power base from which they can bring about needed changes in the colleges and universities involved. Black student organizations on predominantly white campuses have demanded separate living, dining, and office facilities for their members.

Chapter 5

They have called for separate educational facilities and instruction. And, they have demanded standards for college entrance and academic achievement different from those used to measure the academic performance of white students.

Negro college campuses have been spared Black student demands for separate facilities and instruction, because whites are an extremely small minority on these campuses, if they attend those schools at all. Black students have, however, deluged negro and white administrators at these schools with demands for changes in the substance and character of their educational experiences. Here, the demands represent the students' desires to cast off traditionally accepted standards of what constitutes a "good" and "relevant" negro education.

In 1967 and 1968, then, the Black student revolt switched from an emphasis upon confrontations in segregated areas of American life to the college campus. The schools no longer were merely bases of operations and recruitment, as they had been earlier. Now they had become the main battlegrounds in the struggle. Why this "return to the campus"?

First of all, young Blacks saw the need to qualify for positions and responsibilities traditionally assumed by oppressive whites and negroes in Black communities. If Black people were ever going to think seriously of driving the oppressors and exploiters from their communities, then there had to be qualified and competent Blacks to lead them. Black students, responding to the responsibilities spelled out for them by Malcolm X, Stokely Carmichael, and Rap Brown, altered their priorities, for instance, from an emphasis upon such activities as desegregating lunch counters and housing facilities to preparing themselves to operate new Black businesses and build new Black controlled housing facilities in the Black communities of America.

Second, the Black student of the middle 1960's realized, for the first time, that the educational system in America was far from being the shining ideal that white apologists made it out to be.

To the Black students education in America was now just as racist and oppressive as any other institution in the society. It was clear to him that neither Afro-Americans nor educational institutions in America simply were going to disappear. And since Black students had a responsibility to prepare themselves to lead the Black liberation movement, their first task naturally would be to bring about changes in the educational institution that would enable them to pursue such preparations.

Third, Black students saw themselves as constituting a vanguard elite in the Black liberation struggle. As such, true to the mandate presented to them by H. Rap Brown and others, they had a responsibility to legitimize the political activities and actions of Black people in Black communities and on the "block." This task could best be accomplished not simply by their becoming involved in local community political activities, but by conscious and deliberate efforts to express in their educational endeavors and in their actions their support of and the justifications for political acts carried out by Black people at the local level. To the extent that this was to be accomplished, it was necessary for the Black student to transfer to the campus the same brand of radicalism that hitherto had been confined to exposing inequities and injustices in the society at large.

And last, many Black students turned to the campus as the focus of their political activities in the Black liberation struggle, because they were not yet ready to engage in the types of activities which had either augmented or replaced non-violent action in local Black communities as legitimate means of achieving liberation. Although many students were in full sympathy with the new tactics and gave them, much as they do today, verbal support, they themselves were not yet ready to violently engage police, national guardsmen, and state troopers in armed rebellions. They were not yet ready to employ "any means necessary" to bring about freedom, justice, and equality for Afro-Americans. So they returned to the campus, carrying with them their newly found political sophistication, the frustrations of over half a decade of struggle, and their idealism, which had both waxed and waned during the "integrationist" phase of the movement.

What awaited them at the various colleges and universities? What would confront them? What of Black Power, and how would it be realized on predominantly white campuses?

Separation or "self-imposed segregation"

Many educational administrators, faculty members, and concerned citizens—as well as traditionalist, old-line negro civil rights leaders—are frightened, confused, and intimidated by the widespread demands of Black students for separate facilities and, in general, for the institutionalization of a life style separate from that enjoyed by white students on the predominantly white campus. No less confounding to many are the demands of Black students on negro campuses for Black studies programs and Black cultural facilities. These demands are both justifiable and necessary within the context of the present phase of the Black student revolt. And those who refuse to recognize these justifications and the need for separatism are either ignorant of the Black experience in America or are completely out of touch with the realities of the Black liberation struggle in the 1960's, or both.

For the Black student on the white campus, there is nothing new in being alone with his own kind. Over the years, and since 1954 in particular, while liberal white administrators and faculty members at northern universities have piously slapped themselves on the back and criticized southern segregated white schools, the Black student has known the truth about the Black experience in the "integrated" predominantly white college. The truth of the matter is that even today, fraternities, sororities, extra-curricular activities, and many other facets of life at predominantly white integrated colleges are closed to the Black student. The case of the Black athlete is particularly relevant here. So vicious and widespread has been the racism and injustice in collegiate athletics at predominantly white schools that in 1968 a new front was opened in the Black student revolt, an attack by Black athletes on traditionally racist practices in athletics. (A documentary analysis of this aspect of the more general Black student revolt is presented in Harry Edwards' *The Revolt of the Black Athlete*, Free Press, 1969.) Black students have traditionally eaten alone with their own kind; they have traditionally been assigned to dorm rooms with other Blacks; and they have usually socialized mainly with Blacks on the integrated college campus. Typically, segregation within an obstensibly integrated context has been the rule for the Black student. The fact has been driven home, both subtly and directly, that his presence on the predominantly white campus is primarily maintained at the sufferance of liberal whites and, that beyond this presence, he has little legitimacy—if any—in the college community. In short, the call for a separate community of Black students within the larger academic community may be new to the liberal campus in its political implications, but it most certainly is not new in its visible manifestations. For even on the most highly integrated and liberal college campuses, there have always been a Black community and a white community. The Black student today has simply recognized this central fact and moved to capitalize on it in order to realize the goals of the present phase of the Black liberation struggle.

One of the philosophical bases for the Black student's seemingly sudden advocacy of Black separatism in academia is the fundamental distinction which he makes between separation and segregation. Both the conceptual and operational meanings of segregation are, for the Black student, all too clear. Under a segregated system of human relationships, a dominant group defines the limits and boundaries of acceptable behavior, activities, and aspirations for a subordinate group. This usually has the effect of maintaining or

65

reinforcing those advantages enjoyed by the dominant group in the social order. These advantages become, over a period of time, institutionalized within the fabric of practically every aspect of the society, including the political, economic, social, educational, and even the religious spheres of life. For even on Sundays, it is as if some invisible force surged through the nation sending whites to one church and Blacks to another. The results for the subordinate group are usually disastrous—culturally, economically, and politically. Its members, in fact, become inferior, not because they are innately so, but because they are defined as such by their oppressors—and, ultimately, they come to regard themselves as inferior. The subordinate group becomes inferior because its members are treated categorically as inferiors and because they respond to such treatment from a perspective of inferiority. Segregation, then, *has* produced and perpetuated the inferiority complex which afflicts many people in Black society. But this inferiority complex does not stem solely from the fact that Blacks have not been allowed by their white oppressors to socialize, go to school with, work beside, or otherwise rub elbows with whites. In fact, this contrived inferiority has little to do with the absence of physical intermingling between whites and Blacks. The determining factor in bringing about the inferiority complex, exhibited through both the behavior and attitudes of many in Black society, is the fact that these people have accepted the white racist definition of themselves as having been relegated to a sub-human existence in America because of certain "innately inferior" characteristics supposedly possessed by Black people and not by whites. With Black separatism, an entirely different philosophical perspective is brought to bear on the fact of traditional Black-white estrangement. And, it is this difference which renders separatism different from segregation in both its philosophical and political substance and in its consequences.

Black separatism is neither a manifestation of Black

"racism," a cult of Black superiority, or the evidence of Black people's intentions to "do the same thing to whites that whites have done to Blacks for almost four hundred years." In America, *Black* and *racist* are, first of all, mutually contradictory terms. Second, the entire notion of Black separatism being a cultic movement espousing Black superiority is simply fallacious. And, the idea that Blacks who advocate Black separatism are somehow preparing to reciprocate in kind the injustices and humiliations that whites have traditionally heaped upon Blacks is merely evidence of the truth of the old adage that "the guilty flee when no man pursues."

In the present phase of the Black student movement, the advocacy of separatism means that young Black people today are determined to control all aspects of their own environment—social, political, educational, economic, and otherwise—to the advantage of Black people. Unlike segregation, when a subordinate group separates itself categorically from an oppressive dominant group, the former in effect declares a psychological and social sovereignty and legitimacy beyond any that might be ascribed to it by the latter. Such a subordinate group runs its own affairs; it sets its own standards of acceptable behavior and aspirations; and, from its ranks come the people who will be charged with the responsibility of solving the problems facing that group. But most important, it creates its own definitions of itself and its environment. A group that seeks to separate does not attempt to control and exploit other groups in the social order. For its tactic is separation, not the domination that has been the tactic of the white majority in America relative to Blacks. Neither is separation a goal. It is a means of bringing about freedom and justice for Black people in America. Hopefully, Black separatism will develop a more homogeneous and just society, wherein all men can be free and receive justice under a single set of standards. But America is not such a society now, and this is the reality with which Black people are faced. For

Blacks, there are separate standards for almost everything. It is this revelation which Afro-Americans have finally come to understand.

Most Black students recognize today that Afro-Americans, as was stated in the last chapter, are not merely Americans who happen to be Black. Theirs is a life style and environmental condition which is distinctively different from those of other groups, owing to a uniquely Black heritage of slavery, oppression, exploitation, and dehumanization stemming from racism. As such, the problems faced by Blacks are not amenable to solutions typically employed by other groups in overcoming problems issuing from attempts to ascend the socio-economic and political ladders of the system. Black people have been *in* America longer than 95% of all of the other ethnic groups represented in this society, and still they lie at the bottom. In short, they are still not *of* America. In separatism, Black students see a potentiality for developing the Black communities of America into such an internally controlled power block that Blacks will in fact be able to compete on an equal basis with other groups in the larger society. On an individual level, separatism holds the potential for instilling Black people with the pride and confidence necessary if they are to seek self-fulfillment in America. This aspect of Black separatism is all the more laudable because the possibility of societal disaster being precipitated from within remains a definite reality while members of any group feel themselves to be categorically denied the right to such self-actualization.

Separatism on the campus

There are several basic justifications for the advocacy of Black separatism on the college campus. (One of these in particular, the justification for separate educational instruction, will only be mentioned here, but will be discussed in depth in a later chapter.) Calls for Black separatism have run the gamut from demands for separate Black dining facilities and parking lots to cries for separate Black instructional facilities and curricula. Although the specific justification for some of these demands may be peculiar to certain campus atmospheres and conditions, several do conform to philosophical mandates generally accepted throughout the Black student movement.

Today there is considerable evidence to support the assertion that the substance and functioning of traditionally accepted educational activities in America are de facto racist. As such, the educational experiences of Blacks emerge not only as irrelevant—a charge often made by white students—but also as intellectually degrading and racially derogatory. Consequently, Black students have moved to bring about changes that they feel promise more relevant educational experiences as these relate to solving the problems faced by the Black masses in America.

Across America, Blacks have demanded separate educational facilities. Here, the justification is simple. When Blacks and whites have engaged in conversation or discussion about problems facing Black people, there has always been a great deal of discussion back and forth but very little has been resolved. Black students recognize this. They feel that in the latter half of the 1960's, it is a waste of precious time to argue with whites about a fact of the Black experience in America that even a six-year-old Black child would consider trivial or obvious. So rather than waste time arguing with whites about whether or not racism exists in the north, or about whether the racial question revolves around a "negro problem" or a white problem, or about whether Blacks want integration in order to facilitate access to white women, Black students have merely demanded that they be provided with separate educational facilities. The assumption here is that such separate instruction would allow them to move at their own pace toward realizing as much as they possibly can in their pursuit of a relevant education. And this can be done only without the burden of white classmates, who can neither fully understand nor accurately analyze life in America from the Black perspective.

Much the same argument underlies Black student demands for courses taught by Black instructors. They feel that at the present time neither negro nor white professors, no matter how liberal, can capably and competently teach substantive courses relevant to Black people. Each has too much of a stake in and is too much involved with maintaining the racist status quo in the society. Moreover, neither the negro nor the white teacher understands the Black communities of America. The orientations and perspectives of both have been antithetical to or ignorant of the life styles of Black society. The white professor gains his perspectives of Black people, or lack of same, through racist infested socialization and educational processes. The negro often works hard and deliberately to shed all traces of his Black heritage and perspectives and ignores the existence of Black people. To him, the Black community and its problems are merely isolated, academic facts. Realizing the situation, Black students have demanded that Black professors be hired, with students having some decision-making power in determining which professors are Black and which are negro. Such decisions are usually based upon a particular prospect's reputation, his political activities, the content and character of his writings, and/or the tenor of any pronouncements he may have made prior to his being hired.

Black students have been just as adamant in demanding separate housing and dining facilities on campus. For many years at predominantly white colleges, Black students have literally been used both by white students and faculty members as resource items and informants on almost every aspect of Black life in America. It was not until relatively recently, however, that Blacks realized that they were being used this way by whites who usually have had only a casual interest in solving problems of racism and injustice. In the past, Black students have thought nothing of explaining time-and-time again, over and over, to whites how it feels to be discriminated against or abused by racists. They have wasted hours attempting to "justify" various past civil rights protests and rebellions to whites who had demonstrated little concern about racial injustice until Blacks became aggressive in their liberation efforts. Today, however, Black students are rebelling against this kind of exploitation. They realize that the average white person neither understands nor can truly empathize with the Black masses. And what is more, he is not prepared to accept and act upon Black assessments of life in America even after they have been explained to him.

In line with their new sense of racial and cultural pride, Black students have demanded separate living and dining facilities in order that they might pursue and develop a greater appreciation for their own culture, uninhibited by the constant presence of whites, who can neither understand nor contribute to such an understanding. Blacks in America eat different food, so why subject whites to what has been done to Blacks—that is, subject them to a constant diet which may seem bland or distasteful to them? Why subject whites to ethnocentric styles of behavior, dancing, conversation, and attire, which they may not appreciate or identify with and which they may regard as derogatory, vulgar, or uncouth? Black students have tried to avoid these consequences, not out of a hatred for whites, but out of a determination to pursue what is relevant to Blacks.

If separatism is so desirable, then, why go to a predominantly white school in the first place?

Why black separatism on the predominantly white campus?

Since it became clear that Black separatism was to be the central trend on the predominantly white college campuses of America, many have asked why Blacks attend such schools and then seek a separate existence. First, predominantly white schools have the best equipment and facilities available in the educational arena. Unlike negro schools in the south, such institutions of higher learning are not constantly hampered by gross shortages in money, space, and basic educational equipment. And given the magnitude of the problems facing Black society, even the best that American education has to offer may not be sufficient to solve them. So why even consider anything less?

Second, the authorities who control predominantly white schools are not so likely to shut them down in order to stem the political activities of Black students. No such hesitancy constrains the white authorities who run the negro colleges. Here the reprisal is swift—call out the police or shut off the funds. After all, "these kids are only niggers." The authorities used every means at their disposal to keep Columbia University in New York City and San Francisco State College in California open. But predominantly negro Voorhees College in Denmark, South Carolina, was sealed like a tomb. The authorities are extremely wary about using unrestrained force against white students at white schools—as was used against Black students at the negro college in Orangeburg, South Carolina—because often the sons and daughters of important whites attend these colleges and sometimes become involved in confrontations. It is also on the predominantly white campuses of the country—at Cornell, Harvard, Berkeley, Chicago, and the like—that most defense and other types of "vital" research are carried on. Civic and university authorities are not likely to shut these facilities down and set the university off limits to students, some of whom are graduate research assistants working on government projects, simply to curtail the political activities of Black students. This is especially true because, as was brought out in a study in May of 1969, Black students comprise less than 2% of the student populations at the nation's eighty largest and most prestigious universities. Black students recognize these facts and therefore not only apply for admittance to predominantly white schools but stay on and carry out their political activities there. The administrators at such schools are thus forced either to meet the demands of Black students or face continual disruptions and confrontations.

Third, a Black student can be "Blacker" at a predominantly white college than at a negro school. Administrators at negro schools are, typically, middle-class in orientation and appointed or controlled by conservative or racist white government officials or boards of trustees. As such, they tend to assume the position of "overseer" at the negro college to see to it that nothing distinguishably "Black" occurs and that the school continues to produce "responsible" and "respectable" negroes. At the negro school, then, there is usually a deliberate effort made to guard against the possibility that anything in the educational process will be relevant to Black people. At the predominantly white schools, such is not the case. The administrators at these schools are usually unaware of what is relevant to Blacks. Most have not the foggiest notion of what Black students mean by a "relevant education." Such notions as a relevant education for Blacks in the context of a predominantly white school have simply never crossed their minds. Under these circumstances, the Black student is much freer to engage in distinguishably Black activities on the predominantly white campus than at the negro school.

And, last, but by no means least, Black students recognize that Afro-Americans are and always will be surrounded by whites as long as they remain in America. To this extent, the close, homogeneous environment offered by the negro college is artificial and unreal. At the predominantly white college, the Black student functions in a situation more closely representative of that which awaits him in the society at large— a minority of Blacks engulfed by a majority of whites who are often hostile, seldom understanding, and almost always racist.

THE RELUCTANT
REVOLUTIONARIES

Since the Fall of 1967, many whites and negroes in America have accepted the image of the politically active Black student as he has been portrayed in the mass media—a bearded, doped-up, wooly-headed, bead-wearing savage with a gun in one hand and a molotov cocktail in the other who is dead set on burning the colleges and universities of America to the ground to secure relatively insignificant gains or simply to see them burn. The picture had changed since the late 1950's and early '60's when many people, whites in particular, regarded Blacks as innately non-violent, Bible-quoting, childlike figures, striving to be recognized as full-fledged human beings. Needless to say, the latter image is just as distorted as the former. In the Black student movement today, there exist several distinct and sometimes conflicting political perspectives among the active participants in the student revolt. And although for the most part each of these perspectives is legitimate in terms of reflecting the philosophies and ideas of one noted Black leader or another, they nonetheless vary in certain significant respects. On one point, however—the matter of goals—there is virtually unanimous agreement. There is little or no argument over whether freedom, justice, and equality are desirable for Blacks in America. (Any argument that might develop over goals usually centers around the concept of "equality." For many activists in the Black student revolt are not certain that they would even want to be "equal" to George Wallace, say, in any sense of the word.) The major and most significant differences within the movement revolve around questions of means and particularly the meaning of Malcolm X's dictum that "any means necessary is justified" in the struggle to achieve Black

Chapter 6

liberation. As yet, the exact dimensions of the answer to these questions are not clear. What is clear among most Black students, however, is the fact that it is both unnecessary and unintelligent to kill a fly with a sledge hammer. But it is equally clear that no one, regardless of how committed and sincere he may be, can drive railroad spikes with a fly swatter. What typically happens is that students involved individually arrive at an assessment of what means they are willing to employ in order to achieve specific and immediate ends. So while the phrase "we will use any means necessary" is honored by all active participants in the revolt, they vary its interpretation according to how they perceive the significance of immediate goals or lack of same. Unfortunately, white and negro administrators and faculty members, who usually are running scared, interpret the phrase to mean that Black students as a group are deliberately set on burning down the house to get rid of the rats. It is this attitude that usually impels college and university authorities to bring police and national guardsmen onto the campuses. By resorting to such overkill tactics, authorities usually succeed only in consolidating the various elements engaged in the Black student revolt. The activists emerge more unified, more radical, and more uncompromising.

The following categories of student types participating in the Black student revolt are developed from qualitative and ethnographic data gathered by the author while lecturing to and organizing Black student groups on over sixty predominantly white college (two-year and four-year schools) and university campuses across America during the three-year period from Summer, 1966 to Summer, 1969. Due to the complex of suspicion which is inherently a part of the movement, systematic gathering of interview data was practically impossible. Also the highly dogmatic responses of students to formally asked questions made the tactic of using a questionnaire or interview schedule rather undesirable. As an alternative, data was gathered by engaging 378 students in informal coversation. A great deal of such conversation was taped. Most, however, was written in part on note pads during the conversation or jotted down immediately after engaging in such a dialogue. Much of these conversations—both of the taped and written types—were augmented by notes drawn from observations of the student subjects within the context of their conversations and activities with their peers. Although the following typologies are certainly ideal and relatively general, the component characteristics of each are sufficiently specific to render each type identifiable in any Black student population.

The participants in the Black student revolt comprise five types: the radical activist, the militant, the revolutionary, the anomic activist, and the conforming negro.

The radical activist

The radical activist is the third smallest group of Black students active in the revolt. Of the 378 students upon whom attention was focused 56 fit this category. These people typically have relatively long histories of activism in the liberation struggle, usually dating back to participation in SNCC activities during that organization's pre—Black Power days Thus they usually are sophisticated in organizing and mobilizing people and have a substantial amount of firsthand experience in confronting entrenched, legally established institutions and authorities.

The radical activist is usually older—both academically and chronologically—than his Black student peers. He may be a senior or graduate student in his middle or late twenties. He usually comes from a middle-class negro family and first entered college by qualifying under traditional or "normal" standards for entry. Sometime early in the course of his undergraduate career, however, his primary goal of getting a college degree became secondary to a growing interest and participation in political activities revolving around the struggle of Black people for freedom and justice. In other words, somewhere along the line, he discovered that he, too, was Black. As he became more and more involved in political activities, his preoccupation with academic goals became tenuous, as did his ties with his middle-class negro parents, who often neither understood nor favored his involvement. Consequently, his academic career, undergraduate and sometimes graduate, was prolonged.

In 1966 and 1967, heeding the call for Black Power, the radical activist Black student returned to the college campus. It was he who spearheaded the shift in areas of confrontation from segregated public facilities to the college campus. It was the radical activist—the former staunchly non-violent activist turned radical by his experiences during the integration-oriented phase of the movement—who brought the messages of Malcolm X, Stokely Carmichael, and others back to the college campuses of America. And, it was he, too, who first began to agitate for and to organize what have come to be known generally as Black student unions.

In the Black student movement, the radical activist is more politically sophisticated at the domestic level, more experienced, and has more organizational ability than any of the other types. For these reasons, during the early organizational lives of Black student organizations, it is usually the radical activists who politicize the members, organize and run most meetings, define political issues, and either occupy themselves or delegate to others positions of authority and power in the organizational hierarchy.

In the truest sense of the word, the radical activist is a politician. He is willing to create and compromise on relatively insignificant issues in order to achieve more significant goals. Looming as somewhat of a vestige of his involvement in the "non-violent" phase of the student movement is his uneasiness about using premeditated violence or destruction as means to be employed in the struggle. He will, however, use such means if he perceives himself as having been pushed to it by authorities in the course of a confrontation. For the radical activist is, basically, a reformer. And except for the fact that he realized the necessity of Black separatism during the current phase of the struggle and is willing to employ means more radical than non-violent direct action, his orientation differs little from the reformist orientation exhibited by him earlier in political activities. He still believes that America, despite her severe afflictions and institutionalized ills, is worth saving. And what is more, he believes that it can be done without resort to wholesale violence and destruction. But for the radical activist, the ultimate determiner of what means will be employed in the Black student movement rests with the authorities who preside over the nation's campuses. If they do not resort to violence and brutality in their dealings with Black people, then he will not respond violently in his dealings with them.

Because of his relative sophistication and skills, then, the radical activist who organizes a Black student union bears the greatest responsibility for conceiving and implementing the functions of that organization. But his success in wrenching compliance from college administrators with two demands in particular, ultimately brings about his dethronement as chief spokesman, strategist, and organizer among Black students on the predominantly white campus. These are the demands for more "liberal" college entrance standards and financial aid for Black students applying for admittance.

Almost without exception, when Black students have demanded more liberal entrance standards and financial aid for Black people applying for admittance to college, they have done so with the intention of opening college doors to the lower classes of Blacks from "hard-core" Black communities. But, with few exceptions, most of the students who have entered college under such programs have been from the negro middle-class. There are three reasons for this.

First of all, Black youths from the lower classes typically are alienated from the entire educational process at a relatively early stage of their educational careers. As a result, they often drop out of school before they obtain a high school diploma—a minimum requirement for college admittance which most predominantly white four-year schools and almost all negro schools are not willing to waive.

Second, despite the more liberal college entrance policies, a lower-class Black often lacks the motivation to go to college, even if he does possess a high school diploma. Neither home life nor the realities of life in the Black communities of America are conducive to fostering an ethic based on deferred gratification. For the masses of Black youth, a much more practical and realistic goal is a low-achievement ceiling and low-paying job. Consequently, they do not even apply to college.

Finally, and related to the last point, mobility and status in hard-core Black communities is not determined by educational achievement or academic excellence. As a matter of fact, in the Black community any male who excels in school is regarded as somewhat effeminate or as a "punk." Therefore, most young people from Black communities are not likely to see the immediate value of continuing what, in many cases, has already been a disastrous educational career.

So, unlike the Black youth from the middle-class negro family, the accumulated hard realities and lessons of over three-hundred and fifty years of brutal oppression have had all too great an impact on the lower classes of Black youth.

Hence, it has not typically been Blacks from the lower classes who have come to colleges via liberalized entrance standards. The overwhelming majority of those who have come have been more young Black people from bourgeois negro middle-class families. And most of these, by and large, have become Black militants or remained apathetic negroes.

The militant

Once the demand for more liberal college entrance standards had increased the number of young Black students on the nation's college campuses, the leadership days of the radical activist were numbered. And under the circumstances, this result was predictable. For these new students emerged mostly as militants. The militant type is by far the most numerous in the Black student movement. Of the student population studied here 154 of 378 emerged as militants. He, too, is a reformer. But he differs from the radical activist in several significant respects. For the militant is the "nouveau noir" of the Black student movement.

First of all, he tends to be younger, both academically and chronologically, than the radical activist, usually an undergraduate in his late teens or early twenties. He typically possesses neither practical experience in dealing with political issues nor any cohesive philosophy that might guide him in moving politically in a manner relevant to the problems of Black people. For he has, in many instances, just recently begun to discover that he himself is Black and not a negro. This being the case, the campus militant at first does no organizing. Rather, militants are organized and politicized by the radical activists and others. Primarily because he has been "turned on to Blackness" by radical activists and others active in the Black student revolt, the militant picks up and freely uses all the current rhetoric of the movement. He also is the type most likely to wear the latest in "African" styles, which afford him a means of exhibiting his militancy both for the sake of his own ego and to intimidate whites. But the militant's first priority remains a college education. Participation in political activities aimed at bringing about relevant changes in the educational process that will facilitate the solving of problems faced by Black people is secondary. Hence, despite his threatening rhetoric and appearance, the militant is not disposed to get involved in any type of action which will jeopardize his educational future, although he may give lip service to such action. He attempts to rationalize this disposition with the claim that he is "going to return to the Black community" to put to work the skills that he masters during his college career. But the fact of the matter is that the militant has not yet completely accepted the philosophy of Black Power. His goal is to force the white racist establishment in America to allow greater mobility for Blacks in the existing social order. His immediate aspirations are for a high-paying job and the best house that he can afford. And while he may certainly choose a job where Blacks are the primary recipients of his services, the militant is by no means enthusiastic about the idea of actually living in a hard-core Black community. In fact, unlike the radical activist and other types who either have had a great deal of experience in working and organizing in the Black communities of America or who are products of those communities, the militant cannot technically "return" to the Black community, because typically he has never lived or worked there. He has typically been "protected" from such experiences by his negro parents, who have maintained very tight control over him. His close ties with his middle-class negro family are continued throughout the militant stage of his political development.

Initially, the militant seldom attends Black student union meetings. And although he may endorse the programs of the organization, he leaves most of their implementation to the radical activist. He almost never volunteers for committees or other positions vital to the functioning of the union. At some point, however, the militant does become more actively involved, usually as a result of some particular issue which catches his fancy or because something develops that threatens his own personal goals. It is at this point that the militant snatches the reins of power from the radical activists.

The militants typically wrestle power from radical activists by means of a crude type of plebiscite. The radical activist gains control of Black student organizations through his proven ability to mobilize and move people toward defined goals. His success in these efforts makes the exercise of this power legitimate. Under the radical activist, a Black student union functions as sort of a benevolent dictatorship. When

81

the militants take power, however, democratic rule, with all its necessary, but monotonously slow, rules of order and regulations, replaces the efficiency and speed of the radical activist's one-man decision-making authority.

With the militant at the helm, means become less radical, the immediate issues around which he organizes programs of action become less relevant to the Black community, and a premium is placed upon threatening rhetoric and cultural exhibitionism while meaningful political action of significance in achieving the long-range goals of freedom and justice for the Black masses is minimized. In adopting such tactics, militants seek both to participate in the Black student movement and simultaneously to protect their own personal educational goals. But straddling this fence is not an easy task, because constant pressures tend to push militants toward more radical action. These pressures arise from several sources.

First of all, the activities of Black activists on other campuses magnify the timidity of the militants' position and make them realize the relative indefensibility of their would-be political stance within the present context of the Black student movement. Today one of the most insulting remarks that can be made to a Black student attending a predominantly white school is that Black students on his campus have been so "good" that it is not generally known that his is an "integrated" college. In other words, the Black student organization on his campus could not have been doing much that was relevant to Black people, because if it had, other Black student groups would have heard of it.

Second, pressures come from other types of Black students active in the movement. The revolutionary Black students and the anomic activists, as well as the radical activists, force the militants to run the Black student organizations in a more politically relevant fashion. The revolutionary's views about what is politically relevant to Black society are quite different from the militant's, as are those of the anomic activist. It is they, the revolutionaries and anomic activists, who have basically captured the attention of a sensationalist-oriented, white controlled mass media and in doing so have set the standard by which the political relevance of Black student groups is assessed by Black students.

Third, pressures are inadvertently brought to bear upon militants by threatened and intimidated college administrators, civil authorities, and faculty members, who usually take militants more seriously than the militants take themselves. By taking a hard stand on relatively minor issues, campus and civil authorities force the militants to back up radical talk with radical action. And beset by other pressures, militants usually, but reluctantly, oblige such authorities.

Despite the relatively self-deceiving character of the Black militant's political stance, the militant phase of his participation in the struggle passes as he gains more experience, spends more time in the academic arena, and inevitably becomes more involved in the Black student revolt. Aiding the process are the pressures we have already mentioned. He usually becomes more radical and may even become revolutionary. As such, his political perspectives come to approximate those of the radical activist or, less frequently, those of the revolutionary Black student.

The revolutionary

There are few revolutionaries in the Black student revolt and in the broader Black liberation struggle. But the significance of the revolutionary political perspective is not determined by the relative numerical strength of its adherents. For what the revolutionaries lack in numbers, they make up in zeal.

The revolutionaries are the second smallest group active in the Black student revolt, only 47 of the 378 Black students studied here. Like the radical activists and the militants they place a high value on Black pride, on Afro-America's cultural and historical ties with Africa, and on re-affirming the contributions that Black people have made to the growth of America. But, unlike the radical activists and militants, the revolutionaries repudiate almost all means except premeditated and calculated violence as legitimate tactics in the Black liberation struggle. In fact, the Black revolutionary is as far to the political left of the radical activist and the militant regarding tactics as the latter two groups are to the left of traditional negro leaders on the issues of Black separatism and non-violence. It is the revolutionary who has both popularized and who staunchly believes in the implications of the statement that "more political solutions have come from the barrels of guns than from the halls of the united states congress." But, the revolutionary Black student is also unique in other respects.

The socio-economic class origins of the revolutionary seem not to conform to any distinguishable pattern. He may come from either the lower classes of Black society or from the negro middle-class. Of all the types discussed here, he is the most well read and also the most dogmatically ideological. Although he not infrequently has had some firsthand experience in the integration-oriented phase of the Black liberation struggle, he usually has become alienated from the more traditional directions and slow pace of the movement.

The academic and chronological variables of age also tend to defy easy categorization as far as the revolutionary is concerned. He may be among the youngest Black students active in the revolt or he may be among the oldest. But, usually, the older he is, academically and/or chronologically, the more adamant, the more ideologically dogmatic, and the more dedicated he is to the notion that only violent revolutionary upheaval can achieve true liberation for Black people in America. For the revolutionary, unlike the militant and the radical activist, is not a reformer. He holds that Blacks cannot liberate Black society either through non-violent, direct action or through shrewd, political maneuvers calculated to reform. In his way of thinking, the entire institutional structure of America must be totally and irreversibly destroyed, so great is the depth of the nation's corruption, oppressive tendencies, and racist orientation. Unlike the radical activist and the militant, who pursue traditional academic goals while simultaneously trying to bring about changes from within the educational institution, the revolutionary relies chiefly upon self-education as his main avenue of intellectual development. He distrusts much more than the radical activist and militant both the motives for and the content of more established educational curricula. Graduation from college, for him, means little. For of what value is a college degree from a school which has functioned as a major component of a racist and oppressive society when that society is inevitably going to be destroyed? The chief justification for the revolutionary being in college is that the educational institutions of America provide him with a forum and a stage from which to politicize other young Black people. Because he is typically well read, articulate, and usually enrolls only in those courses which interst him politically, he does well in school. However he makes little progress toward fulfilling the course requirements for graduation and thus he tends to become a "professional student." He feels that it is essentially from the ranks of Black students that the intellectual and analytical skills will come which are so necessary to mounting a successful revolution. In short, the revolutionary sees it as no coincidence that the world's most successful modern revolutionaries—Che Guevara, Mao Tse Tung, and Fidel Castro, among others—were all students at the time that they began to formulate their revolutionary ideologies.

Like the radical activist, the revolutionary may enter college under more traditional entrance standards. For he is often adept at both reading and writing, the two basic guides to assessing the potential of prospective college students. But he may also enter college under more liberalized minority group entrance standards.

The revolutionary tends to break off all ties with his

family if he is from the negro middle-class, for the political and social perspectives of his negro parents relative to the masses of Black people are repugnant to him. If he is from the lower classes of Black society, his family ties tend to be lax anyway, because his family, and his parents in particular, can neither discuss with him nor understand the political, intellectual, and analytical foundations of his revolutionary attitudes and actions. In both cases, however, he soon loses almost all contact with his family, and for extended periods of time his parents may know neither of his whereabouts nor of his activities.

Because of his devotion to revolutionary ideologies and dogmatic dedication to the ideas of men such as Malcolm X, Huey Newton, and Stokely Carmichael, the revolutionary student tends to be somewhat of an internationalist. Unlike the militant and the radical activist, who see a possibility for reforming America's institutional structure in order to save the Black masses, the revolutionary believes it necessary to destroy America in order to make the world safe—not only for Afro-Americans, but for all non-white peoples. The revolutionary sees America not only as domestically oppressive, but as the major power oppressing and thwarting the efforts of peoples around the earth to escape from colonialism, exploitation, and racist white domination. Because of his internationalist perspective, the revolutionary often makes the mistake of dogmatically accepting revolutionary philosophies and tactics which have been successful in developing agrarian societies as applicable to the highly urbanized and industrialized societal conditions under which Black people live in America. And from the perspective of many Blacks who listen to his hymn of violent revolution, herein lies the Achilles heel of the revolutionary's entire argument. As one young militant stated, "Russia and China combined would form the most powerful military force in the world and even they are not attacking the U.S.A. I'd be a fool to get out there with *a* pistol or *a* rifle and try to overthrow this country violently."

In the Black student organization, the revolutionary seldom becomes active until a crisis arises. For the deliberately slow pace and politically dubious orientation of organizational activities and programs are often intolerable for him. He agitates among and prods Black student union members and elected militant leaders to become more radical. The revolutionary is seldom elected to positions of authority in the Black student organization, and when he is his tenure in office is usually short-lived. For he tends to push the militant membership at too fast a pace and in too radical a direction to suit the political fancies of the militants. But once a crisis arises, particularly under circumstances where campus authorities have threatened to call in police, and violence against Black student union members seems imminent, the militants often turn to the revolutionary for advice on tactics and strategies for self-defense. If such tactics of self-defense are deemed by the militant majority as insufficient in the face of mounting police power and brutality, they may turn over all decision-making authority to the revolutionary and leave it to him to decide the best strategy for dealing with the police. In such cases, the end product of revolutionary leadership is usually revolutionary action—the burning and bombing of college buildings and offices and armed confrontations between police and Black students. Usually, the most powerful force that impels militants either to overtly or covertly relinquish control of Black student organizations to the Black revolutionary is the fact that college administrators and civil authorities usually resort to overkill tactics in the face of relatively insignificant militant threats.

The revolutionary, regardless of whether he originates from the lower classes of Black society or from the negro middle-class, knows Black people and the Black community. Although it is from among the Black students of the nation that he hopes to draw the necessary intellectual inspiration to mount a revolution, it is from among the ranks of the oppressed and angry lower classes of Blacks that he hopes to draw the soldiers who will destroy America through the use of violent force. Typical of the prospects for this revolutionary army is the Black anomic activist.

The anomic activist

The Black anomic activist is the epitome of the "rebel without a cause." At least he is not conscious of the exact dimensions of his cause. He is simply in a state of rebellion against America and his position in the nation. But nevertheless, he has a role—and a very vital role—to play in the Black student revolt. Numerically, the anomic activist type of Black student is the least represented type in the Black student revolt (only 22 of the 378 students studied here.) However, like the revolutionary, what the anomic activist lacks in numerical strength he more than makes up for by his zeal for radical action. He, like the revolutionary, has been made the stereotype for the Black student by sensation-seeking, white journalists.

The anomic activist, more so than any of the other types we have mentioned, is a product of the naked and unadulterated Black experience in America. Before arriving on the college campus, he may have belonged to one of the thousands of juvenile gangs which proliferate in the Black communities of America. He may also have been charged with several juvenile crimes by the police in his home town. For him, his secondary education was irrelevant both to his future and his then current activities. He usually managed to win a high school diploma because of compulsory attendance regulations, the fact that he did passable work in school, parental pressure to remain in school or leave home, and the fact that his teachers were usually only too happy to see him "graduate" just to get rid of him.

The anomic activist usually applies to colleges near his home, after being prodded by both radical activists and militants to continue his education. But the arguments they use are quite different from the ones that usually are employed to convince students of the benefits of a college education. For in the mind of the anomic activist, a high paying job, high status, and a big, luxurious house are beyond his reach. What lures him is the argument that by going to college, he can prepare himself for a vital role in the Black liberation struggle. In essence then, he is convinced that his people need him. And, the anomic activist is as caught up in the turbulence and rhetoric of the Black liberation struggle as are other Black people. He has always known that he was Black, because the realities of life in America have constantly and persistently driven that single fact home to him—sometimes subtly, often harshly and overtly, but always unequivocably. So the anomic activist applies for admission to college, and under one liberalized admission standard or another, his non-committal references emit just enough of a glimmering of college potential for him to matriculate, usually on a provisional basis.

He is now in college, but educational achievement and graduation are of scant significance to the anomic activist. For everything in his background militates against his developing a set of values based upon such goals. Furthermore, as a result of his earlier educational experiences, he has long since given up any hope or belief that he has the capacity ever to do well in school. For these reasons, the often-heard charge that education in America's colleges is irrelevant to the interest of Black people, despite the degree of its actual truth or falsity, provides a handy rationalization for the anomic activist in his attempts to justify his poor academic performance. So deprived of affection, security, and dignity in society at large, and having taken to the streets to find some meaning in life through gang activities and acts of delinquency, the anomic activist finds himself in a completely alien educational environment.

The anomic activist is typically among the youngest participants in the Black student movement, both academically and chronologically. His academic immaturity tends to be perpetuated by the fact that he typically makes little progress up the academic ladder from freshman to senior or graduate status, partly because he does poorly scholastically but also because he is not hesitant about leaving one school and enrolling in another. When he does so, he usually finds that many of his poor grades are not transferable. Or, he may apply to a school and simply not admit that he had been enrolled previously at another four-year institution. Whether he loses or retains his hard-earned academic credits is of little concern to him, because he feels that he has little stake in either the educational process or in the functioning of any particular college. And his tendency to leave one college and enroll in another is made easy by liberal admissions policies for prospective Black students and financial aid programs.

There are several reasons why the anomic activist moves from college to college. First of all, his life style does not emphasize steady performance over an extended period of time. Second, his erratic educational performance subjects him to criticism and pressure to improve and the threat of dismissal is constantly with him. So to avoid the "flack" and to hasten the inevitable, he simply withdraws from school voluntarily. Third, the anomic activist often perceives other participants in the Black student revolt negatively. To him, the militant is bourgeois and hypocritical, the revolutionary is too hung up on words and ideology, and the radical activist is too analytical and too concerned about planning and calculating each organizational activity down to the last detail.

But the major cause of the anomic activist's moving from college to college is his action orientation. So compelling is this force that he may leave one college at which he is formally enrolled and go to another without formally enrolling at all simply because on the new campus a crisis either is brewing or has already erupted, while at the one he has left things may be relatively calm. In short, the anomic activist follows the crises arising out of Black student activities. And in a state such as California, where there may be politically active Black students on six or seven college or university campuses, all within fifteen or twenty miles of one another, his task of moving from one campus crisis situation to another is made relatively easy.

Within Black student organizations, the anomic activist's almost compulsive orientation toward action and rebellion is the determining factor in his activities. He seldom attends organizational meetings and almost never holds any position of authority. He is usually apathetic about the activities and functions of such groups until a crisis arises. He is seldom concerned about the relative importance of issues. Rarely does he take the time to analyze them. Means-ends relationships or goal-directed action are irrelevant. He is always prepared to take the "whole trip" regardless of the issues involved or the consequences of his actions. He would as soon burn down a college as not. In short, his behavior within the context of the Black student revolt is systematically functional but individually aberrant. Usually, the militant majority active in Black student organizations can effectively suppress and may even denounce the anomic activist. But he becomes an extremely valuable "brother" in crisis situations when police power is brought brutally and forcefully to bear upon Black students.

As we mentioned earlier, the militants may turn to the revolutionaries for advice or leadership in crisis situations. If self-defense tactics clearly are inadequate, the revolutionaries assume complete authority and decision-making power in the group and offensive action becomes the prime means of retaliating against the police. The individuals who carry out the most radical measures are the anomic activists.

Unlike the revolutionary, the anomic activist adheres to no coherent, philosophical ideology. Virtually his entire existence has been marked by diffuse anger and rage. So when campus and civil authorities react to more restrained Black student activities with overkill responses born of ignorance, racist attitudes, and conservative or reactionary traditional-ism, they inadvertently fan to life the anomic activist's smouldering hate and fury. Violence follows, against college communities and facilities. There is literally no limit to the means which the anomic activist is willing to employ, given access to an appropriate arsenal and knowledge of how to utilize it. He can sit-in, disrupt gatherings, commit arson, or bomb as he feels the occasion may demand. But usually the more radical and direct the means employed, the more likely he is to become involved in their implementation.

The anomic activist usually has virtually no ties with his family. Coming from hard-core Black society and often from a single-parent, multiple-sibling family, the tight-knit, tradi-tional, nuclear family style of life has never been a reality for him. In a very real sense, his "family" has always been his peer group on the "block"—that frustrated, angry, and dis-inherited group in Black society from whose ranks come the thousands who yearly fill the nation's alcoholic and narcotics hospital wards and local, state, and federal prisons.

So the anomic activists have finally achieved the relevance and purpose which they have so often sought in the greater society—as the shock troopers of the present phase of the Black student revolt. Drawing guidance from the Black stu-dent revolutionary and legitimacy from the exaggerated re-sponses of college and civil authorities, he has at long last found a relevant role in life.

The conforming negro

The type of student termed here the conforming negro constitutes the second largest group of participants in the Black student revolt, ninety-eight out of the 378 students studied. But the participation of the conforming negro is not of his own choosing. Unlike the other types of Black students we have discussed, his is a passive role in the struggle. His relevance to the Black student movement comes about as a result of the tendency among his white student peers, his professors, and college adminstrators to see all young Black students in the same light. As a result of their preconceived images—images which are created primarily by the white-controlled mass media—these whites tend to lump the conforming negro student together politically with the militant, the radical activist, the revolutionary, and the anomic activist, whom they also perceive as being of one uniform disposition. Nothing could be more erroneous. Actually, the conforming negro is often more critical of the activities of the activists and feels more threatened by them than do whites. There are a number of reasons why conforming negroes act and feel the way they do.

The conforming negro student most closely epitomizes the philosophies, values, and attitudes of the traditional middle-class negroes we discussed earlier in this book, although this type of student does not usually come from a middle-class background. His family most likely has existed on the fringes of the socio-economic boundaries that separate the lower-middle class from the lower classes in Black society. He usually comes from a "respectable," hard-working, church-affiliated family, which has managed to survive just above the poverty level. He generally has completed high school with decent grades and may have spent the first few years immediately following high school graduation working at some unskilled job or fulfilling his military "obligations." But with the liberalization of college admittance standards and readily available financial aid, an opportunity for him to obtain a college education has opened up, and he has taken it.

If two words can capture the essence of the conforming negro's life style on the college campus, those words are "individual achiever." His sole purposes for being in college are to obtain a college degree and, hopefully, at least the rudiments of the educational expertise which that degree supposedly symbolizes. He may be the only person in the history of his family ever to finish high school, and the first person in his community ever to attend college. As a result of these distinctions, he is usually a source of pride to his parents and a special person in his neighborhood. He thus feels an obligation to his parents, to his community, and to himself to complete college. Hence, he perceives himself as having a stake in the maintenance of the established educational institution in America as it now functions. His long-term goals center upon getting a high-paying job and buying a big house, preferably outside of the Black community. He makes no pretensions about returning to the Black community from which he came. For unlike the militant, the conforming negro is blatantly honest about his intentions and goals.

Thus, for the reasons we have just listed, the conforming negro is highly critical of the activities of the other Black students on campus. For they could and often do disrupt class schedules and sometimes close the college completely. In either case, the conforming negro recognizes that such activities could extend his college career beyond the timetable which he has outlined for himself. And then, too, as one such student stated recently at Cornell University, the activities of militant Black students "make all negroes look bad." He failed to complete his statement, which would have revealed what he really meant—that Black students make all negroes look bad in the eyes of white people. And this omission perhaps says more about the conforming negro than does his conformity to the traditional negro role and orientation and lack of concern about the plight of the masses of Afro-Americans. He never criticizes white or negro college administrators or civil authorities for their intransigence on issues which clearly must be changed if Black people are to receive a relevant education. He is usually too busy being appreciative toward whites for being permitted to attend "their" college.

The conforming negro adheres to no philosophy other than that passed on to him by his parents and other traditional socialization agents of the society. His immediate activities

are guided almost completely by his own individual achievement motivations. His ties with his family are extremely close
and extremely strong. For by continually assessing their
position in America, he can gauge the rate of his own progress
and mobility up the socio-economic ladder. In his mind, he
knows where he is going, and his parents and family provide
him with evidence of how far he has come.

The conforming negro attends no Black student organization meetings on his campus and is usually ostracized by
Blacks who do—as are all proven and discernible negroes. As
a result, the conforming negro student typically associates
only with whites or with other negroes. Today, more than
at any other time in history, young whites, in particular, are
only too happy to dine, date, and otherwise fraternize with
negroes, given the fact that Black people are advocating Black
separatism. (Whites are funny that way. When Blacks were
begging to "integrate" with whites, the whites were saying
that integration takes time and that Blacks must not move
too fast. Now that Blacks are advocating separation, there
are not enough negroes on most predominantly white campuses, nor in the general society, to go around.)

Despite the fact that he is typically lumped together with
Black college students by whites, the conforming negro, upon
occasion, serves a useful purpose for the white establishment.
Sometimes he publicly denounces the activities of Black students in the mass media, particularly on television, and this
helps to create the fallacy that such activities are the work
of a few radical malcontents and that the majority of Black
students are appalled by such acts and repudiate them. And,
the conforming negro does not always commit this act out of
ignorance of the truth. Often he knows all too well the nature
of his deed. Under such circumstances, his conformity to traditional standards for negro behavior degenerates to what
amounts to treason against his peers.

These, then, are the five major types of students participating, passively or actively, in the current phase of the

Black student revolt. A sixth category was not included in these extended discussions because its members are insignificant in both number and relevance to the revolt, and thus bear only mention here. This category is comprised of students from upper-class negro families. These are the sons and daughters of elected or appointed local, state, and national negro government officials; of well-known negro celebrities; and of other known miscellaneous negro personalities. Like the conforming negro, the student coming from the negro upper-class demonstrates little concern himself about the plight of the masses of Blacks nor is he openly sympathetic with the efforts of Black students who are. Because of the notoriety or social standing of his family, however, whites seldom make the mistake of lumping him together with the other types, as they often do in the case of the conforming negro. Under such circumstances, the upper-class negro student is denied the role of even a passive and involuntary participant in the Black student revolt.

DIALOGUES OF REVOLT, COOPERATION, AND APATHY

The purpose of this chapter is to present statements which typify the attitudes of subjects from each of the five categories of students discussed in the preceding chapter. These statements are taken from the same information out of which the typologies were developed. The statements presented here are those which are felt to most accurately represent the philosophical and political dispositions of students in each of the five categories.

The following statements were in response to questions dealing with nine major issues about which Black students are concerned today on predominantly white campuses. These issues are those of (1) separate housing and dining facilities; (2) separate Black curricula; (3) separate instructional accommodations and facilities; (4) the hiring of Black faculty; (5) legitimate means for achieving immediate and long range goals; (6) Black-white coalitions; (7) increases in the admission of Black students; (8) the presence of military recruiters and recruiters representing industries and other business enterprises which are considered by Black students to be major perpetrators or perpetuators of domestic and/or international racism and injustice; (9) and, the rebellions of Black athletes on college campuses. The statements selected did not all come from a single student from each of the categories. Rather, the statements were selected from the responses of many students from each of the five types. The questions asked of the students precedes the selected repre-

Chapter 7

sentative responses of students on each of the issues outlined above. The names of students used are not necessarily those of the actual interviewees, but the institutional affiliations indicated are valid, as are the other data.

I. WHAT ARE YOUR FEELINGS ABOUT SEPARATE
HOUSING AND DINING FACILITIES FOR
BLACK STUDENTS?

James, 20, junior, a militant at San Francisco State College, California:

It is not only desirable that we [Blacks] have separate living and eating facilities, it is imperative if we are to survive in this society. We must have the chance to appreciate our own kind and our own culture. And, you can't do this if, every time you turn around, you are faced with a room full of "crackers." If you live with them, you see them everywhere you turn, from the time you get up until the time you go to bed. Whites have their fraternities and sororities to go to. Negro fraternities and sororities don't serve the interests of Black people; therefore, we must have our own Black houses or co-ops, so that we, too, can get off to ourselves and discuss and appreciate that which is of interest and relevance to us—undeterred by either whites or negroes.

Cecil, 26, first-year graduate, a radical activist at California State College at Los Angeles, California:

I feel that separation of Blacks and whites is very necessary in this stage of the struggle. We learned a lot while we were on that "integration treadmill"—more than our white "brothers" learned. We see that there are some things that only Blacks can learn from or teach to Blacks, if the experiences gained are going to be a contribution to the solution of our problems—we are already separate in the nation, so we must begin to organize students to work from the premise that, until things are made better by Black people, we are going to

Dialogues of revolt, cooperation, and apathy

remain outside of the system. Therefore, we must not continue to orient students toward integrating into the system—you know, a few token negroes here, a few there—but they must be made to see the need of returning to the Black community. Because individual Black people can succeed only to the extent that the masses of Blacks are significantly better off, both absolutely and relatively.

Josh, 23, second-year senior, a revolutionary at San Francisco State College, California:

The issue of separate facilities for Black students, in and of itself, is of no significance. The structure of the society is so corrupt that anything which is truly Black *cannot survive unless other revolutionary changes have taken place in the society. This is why the pigs [police] shoot up Black Panther offices, and some pigs actually belong to the N.A.A.C.P. The N.A.A.C.P. is not a Black organization. At best, it is a bourgeois negro escapist's apology for a group whose task it should be to aid in the liberation of the Black masses. The Black Panthers deal with the masses, and they address themselves to the masses and their needs. The establishment, therefore, moves against the Panthers, because the Panthers are a big threat to the perpetuation of racism and oppression.*

So, just because Blacks are separate, this doesn't mean anything. We have always been separated from whites. But, the issue of separatism serves as a good mobilizing incentive, and it also demonstrates that Black people are beginning to think of themselves as outside of the system. And, that is the first step to seeing the system as the enemy and then to destroying it.

George, 19, freshman, an anomic activist at San Francisco City College, California:

I think that we [Blacks] should have what we want. And, the white man is not going to give up anything without a fight. We [are going] to have to take it. If we want separate houses, I think that we are going to have separate houses.

But, we are going to have to take [them] and anything else we want. 'Cause the honkie don't give dirt away.

Mary, 22, junior, a conforming negro at the University of Washington, Seattle, Washington:
     Why should we separate. We have been separate for almost 400 years, because white folks wanted it. Now to get back at them, some [negroes] are asking to be separate themselves. I know whites who I like better than some [negroes]. I think that it is mostly an individual thing. If you don't like a person, then get away from him. If you do, then stay around him. But, to condemn all whites is as bad as whites condemning all [negroes]. Some of my best friends are whites who I live with in the dorm.

II. HOW DO YOU FEEL ABOUT DEMANDS FOR AUTONOMOUS BLACK STUDIES CURRICULA?

Rochelle, 21, junior, a militant at San Jose State College, San Jose, California:
     The [courses] taught here are irrelevant to the goals and interests of Black people. They prepare us and orient us toward moving out of our communities and into white society. Now, we have found out that we are not going to become part of white society any time in the immediate future and, possibly, not even in the long range future. And, the courses don't prepare us to live in Black society and deal with our problems. This is the only way that we can survive as a people [i.e., by having a separate Black curricula which addresses itself to the problems facing the masses of Black people]. Otherwise, we wind up in that marginal, schizophrenic bag that our parents are in. And, I never want to be a negro again.

Bill, 23, junior, a radical activist at Northwestern University, Evanston, Illinois:
     We must have courses that address themselves to the problems faced by Black people just like whites have courses

Dialogues of revolt, cooperation, and apathy

that answer the needs of white America. Black studies and the potential contribution that [lie in the mastering of] these courses is the only [justification for] Black students being on any college campus. Unless we fight for [such courses] and make them a reality, we are functioning in co-operation with a corrupt and racist institution in America. As such, we leave college as negroes and not Black people; and, as negroes, we [become] the enemies of liberation of the Black masses.

Babu, 28, junior, a revolutionary at Columbia University, New York City, New York:

Black studies are not so significant, because the struggle is not going to be won in a classroom. The fight must inevitably involve armed struggle. But, Black studies do show students that in no way can they win the war for Black liberation within [the context of the existing system]. To the extent that real Black studies programs become a reality, then to this same extent, the establishment is going to move to shut these programs down.

Sonny, 21, sophomore, an anomic activist at the University of California at Los Angeles, Los Angeles, California:

I'm for Black studies because they give me the education I need to help my people. Right now I don't even have a major because I don't see anything at this whole damn school that does anything for me. Most of the stuff that they offer may be good for the patty boy, but it don't do nothing for me.

Willie, 23, senior, a conforming negro at the California State Polytechnical College, San Luis Obispo, California:

It seems to me that it is kind of ridiculous. If the courses offered are valid in the society, then why try to separate yourself out from the rest of the college community. I don't understand what all the commotion is all about. I am going to get a good job in San Francisco, making about 8,000 dollars a year, when I leave here. If the education that I am getting here was so irrelevant, I wouldn't be able to get a job. I think that some of these [Black students] are just imitating students at other schools. They just want to be in the spotlight. They want attention, and it doesn't matter to them if it is good or bad. I think that it just goes to show that you can take a nigger out of the ghetto, but you can't take the ghetto out of the nigger. Any administrator who falls for that Black curriculum line doesn't know what he is doing. I would never major in the stuff, because you can't get a job by learning Black literature or Black poetry. These [Black students] are just acting the nigger.

III. WHAT DO YOU THINK ABOUT SEPARATE
INSTRUCTIONAL FACILITIES FOR
BLACK STUDENTS?

Rochelle, 21, junior, a militant at San Jose State College, San Jose, California:

It is necessary for us to have separate Black instruction, because, if whites are in the class, they waste too much time arguing about simple and irrelevant points. They just waste too much time. Their thing is dialogue. Whites don't care if Black problems are solved or not. They dig intellectualism and discussion. And, they are not going to act even after they are convinced of a particular point of action and the need to carry that action out. So, why waste time with honkies. They aren't going back to the Black community. They should be in their own separate courses learning to deal with the causes of the problems [confronting Black people]. And, these [courses] are in the white community. Black education is as irrelevant to whites as white educations have been to Black people."

Bill, 24, senior, a radical activist at the University of Texas at El Paso, El Paso, Texas:

If whites are in a Black class, the whole atmosphere of the classroom changes. Black people are not as free to express

Dialogues of revolt, cooperation, and apathy

themselves and explore all of the problems honestly. You see this all the time. Blacks can be discussing anything relevant to them and the solutions to their problems, and a white cat walks in, and the whole atmosphere changes. Spontaneity is gone. And, whites are the same where Blacks are concerned. One Black cat or negro in a white meeting makes the whole meeting different than if only whites were [present]. Therefore, we can be most effective if only Blacks are in the classroom.

Ike, 21, sophomore revolutionary, University of California at Berkeley, Berkeley, California:
   I don't see where it makes any difference if whites are in the class or not. They are not going to let Black people have total control over the courses, and as long as whites control them, whites may as well be in them. And, anyway, whites can bug the classrooms and hear everything that goes on. Blacks may as well let the devils into the classroom. At least then, they will be able to see them and observe their reactions to what goes on. In any case, the junk is eventually going to leave the classroom and become plans for action to bring down this oppressive society. And, you are not going to be able to sneak a revolution over on honkies. You are going to have to face them with the issues and any action that you have planned in the classroom or anywhere else.

Larry, 21, sophomore, an anomic activist at Indiana University, Bloomington, Indiana:
   I don't think that honkies should be in anything Black. The only thing that crackers can do for us is give us the money and other stuff that we need to do our thing. Anything else they have, they can keep—their sympathy, their ideas, and their damn advice.

Mike, 24, senior, a conforming negro at Luther College, Decorah, Iowa:
   I feel that the best education can be gotten by all mem-

bers of the college being in on the classroom discussions. I wouldn't want to be part of an all Black anything. I am going to be living, working, and doing other things with whites as long as I stay in this country. So, I may as well be with them here. I am against it.

IV. HOW DO YOU FEEL ABOUT HAVING ONLY BLACK INSTRUCTORS TEACHING BLACK COURSES?

John, 23, senior, a militant at the University of Iowa, Iowa City, Iowa:

It is a necessity. I can't learn anything [of importance to Blacks] from a white man. He doesn't know or understand things from the Black perspective. And, he can't teach me what he doesn't know himself.

Gregg, 24, senior, a radical activist at the University of Oregon, Eugene, Oregon:

You cannot have a Black studies program without Black instructors any more than you can make an omelet without eggs. Whites and negroes can't teach us what we must know to solve our problems. Honkies are simply tied into the status quo and negroes are too insecure to tell the truth if they can remember what it is. Black instructors must teach Black courses. Otherwise, you have a situation where the fox is responsible for watching over the safety of the chickens.

Jahid, 27, second-year senior, a revolutionary at Sacramento State College, Sacramento, California:

I'm for Black instructors teaching Black courses—if they are Black. But, if they are, they won't last long, because the racist administration would find some pretext to get them out of the college. Nathan Hare was fired from Howard and is in trouble at San Francisco State, because he is Black and teaches his courses from a Black perspective. A racist and oppressive college, which is nothing but an indoctrinational tool of the oppressive and imperialistic [United States] govern-

ment, has to move on all Black people—regardless of their credentials—in order to maintain the delusion of security. . . .

Doc, 21, sophomore, an anomic activist, at Merritt College, Oakland, California:
 I'm for having Black instructors, because we need them. We just have to push the m.f.'s to the wall to make sure that we get them.

Suzzanne, 23, senior, a conforming negro at the University of New Mexico, Albuquerque, New Mexico:
 I don't care what color the professor is. I am only interested in what he knows and the grade that he gives me. I graduate in June [1968], and all of my grades were given to me by white teachers. They have been fair, and I have liked some and disliked some. My references for graduate school were all written by whites, and they wrote good references. They must have, I was accepted at U.C.L.A. with partial [financial aid]. So, I think the thing to demand is good teachers and not Black, white, or yellow teachers.

V. WHAT DO YOU THINK ARE LEGITIMATE MEANS
 TO BE USED IN ACHIEVING THE IMMEDIATE AND
 LONG-RANGE GOALS OF BLACK PEOPLE?

Ruby, 22, senior, a militant at Wellesley College, Wellesley, Massachusetts:
 I think that any means necessary is justified. We have been in this country for four-hundred years, and we are still on the bottom. The white man told us that we could become a part of america by "Toming" under Booker T. Washington, and we tried it. He told us we could do it by being non-violent, and we tried that. Now, I think it is time that we set our own means. And, how rough and violent we are depends on how low down and racist whites and niggers are in the face of our efforts.

Charles, 22, senior, a radical activist at Syracuse University, Syracuse, New York:

Whites will determine how violent the means of Black liberation [become]. We will be guided by our determination to achieve our goals. If whites and the system force us to it, we will be as violent as we have to be. Any means necessary is legitimate as long as it is intelligently planned. When we start putting ceilings on what we will do, then I think that we also put a ceiling on the amount of liberation we will achieve.

Rodney, 21, junior, a revolutionary at Howard University, Washington, D.C.:

No meaningful goals will be achieved without armed struggle. . . . That's right. Violence! All that happens in all of this political maneuvering and negotiations with the beasts in power is that Black people and Black liberation efforts are co-opted. They are pacified with a few crumbs that honkies are more than willing to give up to keep Blacks quiet and thinking that they are making progress. Crackers can't co-opt revolution, and no revolution, as St. Malcolm said, has ever been non-violent.

Louis, 22, freshman, an anomic activist at the University of California at Los Angeles, Los Angeles, California:

Well, Brother, the means is the whole thing. If you show weakness, then the man just crushes you. If you show him that you will destroy him and his property or that you are willing to take a chance on being destroyed yourself to get certain things, then he is a lot less likely to brutalize you. You have to stand up. I think that there has already been too much talking.

Steven, 24, senior, a conforming negro at Yale University, New Haven, Connecticut:

I don't hold with violence and disruptions. I think that

Dialogues of revolt, cooperation, and apathy

Yale has enough avenues of redress to answer any questions or demands by any student satisfactorily. And, these people . . . [the administrators and faculty] are intelligent people. They understand English. I think that the civil authorities should be called on campus when order breaks down, I don't care what group is guilty.

VI. WHAT IS YOUR OPINION OF THE POTENTIAL FOR BLACK-WHITE COALITIONS IN THE STRUGGLE AGAINST RACISM AND INJUSTICE?

Charley, 19, sophomore, a militant at Luther College, Decorah, Iowa:

There is no place anywhere in the Black liberation struggle for honkies. Just like there is no place in the sheep herd for the wolf. If they really want to help, they can do it within their own groups and in their own communities. They can do it by breaking down some of the barriers that whites have thrown up to Black freedom. But, not inside of our organizations. They can work with us on some issues as long as we determine their actions.

Lois, 26, graduate student, a radical activist at Fresno State College, Fresno, California:

Yes, we can work with whites . . . as long as we control the power and authority. All of it. When whites have come into our organizations or worked with us in the past, they have taken our organizations over and pretty soon we are dancing to their music when we should be fighting for our freedom. So, Black-white coalitions are possible, as long as we control everything. If whites are willing to serve the interest of Black people, then boom! They have a place.

O'dale, 23, senior, a revolutionary at St. Cloud State College, St. Cloud, Minnesota:

Black people must understand that we must join up with

all revolutionaries, regardless of what color they are. But, they must be revolutionaries. I don't know too many white revolutionaries. I know a lot of white radicals and liberals, but very few revolutionaries. Most honkies are just unwilling to attack other honkies or this honkie controlled system. But, if I could deal with a real revolutionary white group or individual, I'd do it. When it comes to revolution, it is the politics that makes the difference and not the skin color. That's why Fidel Castro and Che Guevara are known as revolutionaries, and Ed Brooke is known as a co-opted negro and enemy to Black people.

Willie Lee, 21, sophomore, an anomic activist at the University of Missouri, Kansas City, Missouri:
I don't dig honkies in any way, place, or shape! So, we don't even have to discuss that.

Lucile, 24, senior, a conforming negro at Wellesley College, Wellesley, Massachusetts:
I think that we have to work together with all people. We are just as bad as whites if we discriminate against them. So, I would say that whites can still help in the civil rights movement. It was a mistake to drive white people away [from the struggle]. . . . How do we ever hope to integrate if we segregate ourselves?

VII. WHAT DO YOU THINK ABOUT THE DEMANDS BEING MADE TO INCREASE THE NUMBER OF BLACK STUDENTS ON CAMPUS?

Leon, 23, senior, a militant at Santa Clara University, Santa Clara, California:
In the past, college has been a legitimate goal for mostly just white folks and bourgeois negroes. Now [colleges] must serve Black people. Any Black person who applies for college should be accepted—with a full scholarship.

Dialogues of revolt, cooperation, and apathy

Cyntilla, 28, graduate student, a radical activist at Stanford University, Palo Alto, California:

Every college and university in this country should be open free to any Black person who wants to attend. The white standards for admission don't apply to us, because they function in such a way to keep Black people out. Whites have been telling us for years, "Pull yourselves up by your boot straps." Okay! That's what we are going to do—with or without whites. The doors of the college must be opened wider to Black people, or we must make sure that there is no college which is peaceful enough to give anybody an education.

Ed, 23, junior, a revolutionary at the University of California at Berkeley, Berkeley, California:

I have mixed feelings about the mess. I've seen too many potentially political Brothers and Sisters come to Cal and get sucked into the damn system. They forget about the problems faced by Black people and start going for themselves. If the school has the right political atmosphere, yes, there should be more Blacks. But, if it hasn't, I'd just as soon see Black people stay on the "block," because out there they are not going to be sucked in by intellectual bull. The truth about Black people's position in America is "everyday" out there.

Willie Lee, 21, sophomore, an anomic activist at the University of Missouri, Kansas City, Missouri:

I think that Black people should start their own colleges. To hell with the honkies' schools.

Phil, 24, senior, a conforming negro at Princeton University, Princeton, New Jersey:

I think that anyone who qualifies should be allowed to go to college. I don't think that special programs and standards should be started just for negroes. I do believe that some sort of financial aid for negroes should be worked out, but not special entrance standards. We are just as smart as whites; we just don't have their money. I got in with my grades . . .

from a high school where I had to compete with whites for good grades, but I got in. I just had to work for a year to get enough money to go to college. Once I got in, I did well enough to get a scholarship. Other negroes should do the same thing.

VIII. WHAT DO YOU THINK ABOUT RECRUITERS BEING ON COLLEGE CAMPUSES AND REPRESENTING SUCH ORGANIZATIONS AS THE UNITED STATES MARINE CORPS, DOW CHEMICAL, AND CHASE-MANHATTAN BANK?

Obie, 22, junior, a militant at Cornell University, Ithaca, New York:

I think that Black students have a responsibility to expose any group which is perpetuating racism and oppression in this country or abroad. The United States marines are a bunch of murdering mercenaries. Dow chemical company manufactures the weapons used by the government to commit genocide against the Vietnamese people. And, everyone knows about the relationship between Chase-Manhattan bank and the maintenance of apartheid in the Union of South Africa. Black students should confront the agents of [such organizations] and expose them for what they are.

Richard, 25, senior, a radical activist at Cornell University, Ithaca, New York:

The people who come on campus recruiting for the institutions and organizations which uphold or reinforce racism and injustice should be confronted just as racism and injustice at Cornell has been confronted. How we do this is in the hands of the administration. If the administration can't see how contradictory it is to, say, have Chase-Manhattan bank recruiting on this campus and at the same time tell us that Cornell is against racism and injustice, then we must push Cornell University to the point where its administrators can see the contradiction, and also see that we, as Black people, refuse to tolerate it.

Dialogues of revolt, cooperation, and apathy

Leo, 23, sophomore, a revolutionary at San Mateo City College, San Mateo, California:

It really doesn't make sense to me to drive a few recruiters off of a campus. Suppose that all recruiters were [prohibited] from ever coming on campus again. The companies would still be doing what they are doing. The marines would still be committing genocide in Viet Nam, Detroit, and Newark. Dow would still be making napalm. Until we destroy the system that is supporting and [perpetuating] the marines and Dow chemical company, we may as well be trying to sweep sand off of a beach.

Leroy, 21, freshman, an anomic activist at San Jose State College, San Jose, California:

I think that we should kick every recruiter's butt who comes on this campus. They have no business here. They are our enemies.

Reed, 24, graduate, a conforming negro, Harvard University, Cambridge, Massachusetts:

I think that anyone with legitimate legal business on campus should be allowed to do business at any university. If we start saying who can and who can't come on the campus, based upon the political views of any one or two groups . . . well, where does it end? That sounds too much like nazism to me.

IX. WHAT DO YOU FEEL ABOUT THE REBELLIONS OF BLACK ATHLETES ON COLLEGE CAMPUSES TODAY?

John, 22, senior, a militant at San Jose State College, San Jose, California:

It's long overdue.

Richard, 25, senior, a radical activist at Cornell University, Ithaca, New York:

As far as I am concerned, the thing that happened in the 1968 Olympics should have happened in the 1936 Olympics.

111

I don't believe that there are going to be too many more days of Tomism in athletics.

Charles, 22, junior, a revolutionary at California State College at Los Angeles, Los Angeles, California:
There shouldn't have been any Black people at all in Mexico City in 1968. And, the only reason why Blacks should play pro sports is so that they can channel some of that honkie money back into the Black community to buy guns with and to help support the revolutionary activities of Black people.

Willie Lee, 21, sophomore, an anomic activist at the University of Missouri, Kansas City, Missouri:
We [Black people] have got no time for fun and games. That's part of our problem . . . we like to play too much.

Reed, 24, graduate, a conforming negro, Harvard University, Cambridge, Massachusetts:
I don't see what they are fighting for. Many negroes have moved to respected and high positions in society as a result of athletics. I think that they are cutting off their noses to spite their faces. If I had any athletic ability, I'd do what ever I could to get as much money and prestige as I could get. Bill Russell makes 100,000 dollars a year. What reason would he have to rebel against anything?

Goals and means: a comparative glance

Today, one often hears that America is *moving* toward the development of two distinct societies within her political and geographic boundaries. Nothing could be more erroneous. America has, in fact, existed as a nation split into three societies for almost four-hundred years—one white, one negro, and one Black; one oppressing and two oppressed; one dominant, one condescendingly subordinate, and one struggling for liberation; one free and two enslaved. The crisis in America revolves around the increasingly more apparent fact that the oppressive powers of this nation and their negro counter-

Ideology!

parts must now recognize the third Black social order as a result of the more aggressive stance of more Blacks, some of whom have hitherto existed as negroes. This third social order has traditionally been antithetical to the complementary relationship existing between the white and negro societies. This third social order is what we have referred to as "Black society" throughout this book. Its roots go deeper into America than do those of the negro social order. For as we stated earlier, negroes were created by whites in America. There were no negroes in Africa before the coming of the white man and his technology, his inhumanity, and his oppression. Negroes occur naturally nowhere on earth.

The key distinguishing characteristic that differentiates Black society from the negro social order is the continual struggle Black people have waged for freedom, justice, and dignity. The history of this struggle goes back to the first Blacks who chose suicide rather than slavery. In the wake of the struggle lie the examples set by past generations of Black people and Black leaders. Men and women such as Nat Turner, Sojourner Truth, Malcolm X, Martin Luther King, Jr., and others left this and future generations of Black people poignant examples of both the degree of commitment necessary and the sacrifices which are inherently part of any liberation struggle.

Through its racist and exploitative political, economic, and social policies, this nation created both the negro social order and the negroes to fill its ranks. The negro social order has functioned in an accommodative, condescending, and complementary fashion to the dominant, oppressive, and racist white social order. The upper echelons of the negro social order have never been as high, status-wise, as the upper strata of white society. And, likewise, the doldrums of white society have never been quite so low or disreputable as the lowest elements of the lower classes in the subordinate negro social order. The stratification levels of the two social orders are portrayed in Diagram 1.

Table 1. BLACK STUDENT TYPES: Comparison of Orientations and Political Philosophies

Type	Black Social Order		Subordinate Negro Social Order		Dominant White Social Order	
	Goals	*Any Means Necessary*	*Goals*	*Means*	*Goals*	*Means*
Radical Activist	+>	+	<-	<-	<-	<-
Militant	+>	+	-	<-	+	-
Revolutionary	+>	+>	<-	<-	<-	<-
Anomic Activist	0	+>	-	-	-	-
Apathetic Negro	-	<-	+	+	+>	+>

Diagram 1 RELATIVE LEVELS OF STRATIFICATION

**Stratification of
Subordinate Negro
Society**

**Stratification in
Dominant White
Society**

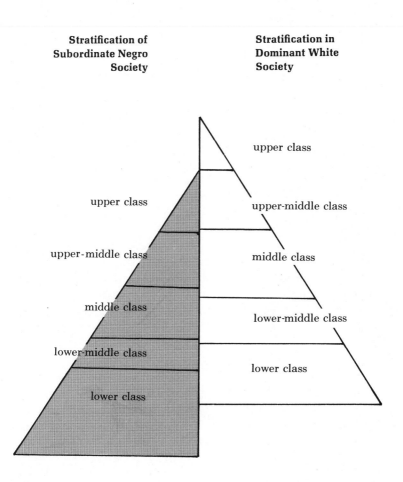

As Diagram 1 indicates, America has established two separate systems of stratification based upon race. Although there are definitely possibilities for mobility within each separate social order, to cross the caste-like boundaries from negro society into white society is extremely difficult, if not impossible, without resorting to "passing" if one is able.

America has established this separation and, indeed, has insisted that it be perpetuated. The sudden concern of federal, state, and local governments with the problems does not arise out of belated recognition of factionalism. (Blacks, whites, and negroes have known for some time that there are really two Americas, one white and the other non-white. Government concern stems from the emergence of a third Black social order. The Black social order, unlike the negro, has not meekly accepted a subordinate, accommodating position relative to the larger society. And therein lies the threat to the status quo which has existed between the negro and dominant white social orders until now.

Table 1 illustrates the various dispositions of each of the five major types participating in the Black student revolt regarding their advocacy of the goals and means of each of the three social orders we have just discussed, and their commitment to them. The signs adjacent to each type signify the following:

+   signifies acceptance of goals and/or means
−   signifies rejection of goals and/or means
<−   signifies rejection and engagement in some form of endeavor to weaken legitimacy of goals and/or means
+>   signifies acceptance and engagement in some form of endeavor to increase or maintain the legitimacy of goals and/or means
0   signifies no commitment to goals and/or means.

By way of further clarification of Table 1, the following statements, pertaining to each type listed, are offered:

Dialogues of revolt, cooperation, and apathy

RADICAL ACTIVIST:

+>   *This sign portrays the radical activist's acceptance of
Black goals and his deliberate efforts to further
legitimate and realize these goals;*

+   *Indicates an acceptance of the dictum that "any
means necessary is justified," but an unease
with more radical and "extreme" means, especially
those involving the use of violence;*

<−   *Indicates a fundamental non-acceptance of both negro
and white goals and means, and deliberate efforts
to neutralize or eliminate totally the legitimacy and
prevalence of such goals and means.*

MILITANT:

+>   *Indicates acceptance of Black goals and deliberate
efforts to realize and further legitimate these for
Black masses. The sign + under white goals
portrays the strains and pressures upon the militant
in his efforts to achieve the "American dream" for
himself and, at the same time, pursue the goals
of Black society;*

+   *Under Black, means, this sign signifies the advocacy
of, but a basic unease with, the more extreme means
which tend to be legitimated by commitment to
the dictum "any means necessary are justified" in
the pursuit of Black liberation;*

<−   *Indicates the militant's non-acceptance of negro goals
and means, and his deliberate efforts to neutralize
or eliminate totally the legitimacy and prevalence of
these in American society;*

−   *Indicates the militant's non-acceptance of dominant
white means without an attendant commitment to*

*neutralize or eliminate the legitimacy and
prevalence of these.*

REVOLUTIONARY:

+> *Indicates the revolutionary's acceptance of Black goals
and means and his commitment to, and deliberate
efforts toward, further legitimating and realizing both;*

<− *Indicates the revolutionary's non-acceptance of both
negro and white means and goals, and his deliberate
efforts to neutralize or eliminate the legitimacy
and prevalence of these.*

ANOMIC ACTIVIST:

0 *Indicates no coherent philosophy or pattern of
attitudes regarding Black goals;*

+> *Indicates the anomic activist's commitment to "any
means necessary" and his preference for use of more
radical means in the Black liberation struggle;*

− *Indicates the anomic activist's non-acceptance of goals
and means of both negro and white social orders,
without attendant goal directed and patterned efforts
to neutralize or eliminate the prevalence and
legitimacy of these.*

CONFORMING NEGRO:

− *Indicates the conforming negro's non-acceptance
of Black goals, without attendant efforts to eliminate
the further legitimacy of these;*

<− *Indicates non-acceptance of Black means and
deliberate efforts to neutralize or eliminate any
existing legitimacy of these;*

Dialogues of revolt, cooperation, and apathy

+   *Indicates an acceptance of negro goals and means,*
        without attendant deliberate efforts to increase
        the legitimacy and prevalence of these;

+>   *Indicates the acceptance of white goals and white*
        means, with attendant deliberate efforts to maintain
        the prevalence and legitimacy of these.

Table 1 shows clearly that the majority of students involved in the Black student revolt today (mostly militants,
radical activists, and conforming negroes) are by no means
dead set on destroying America and its institutions. They are,
basically, reformers. And while Stokely Carmichael's assertion
that "Black people need more revolutionaries and fewer militants, radicals, and negroes" may be true, it is, unfortunately
—or fortunately—depending upon your politics—not Carmichael or people like him who will determine if reform or
revolution will be the prevailing mode of operation. Under the
present circumstances, the chief determiners of this all-im-
portant choice will be America itself and those who control
this nation. And as far as the Black student revolt is concerned, the sincerity and speed with which this nation's institutions of formal education solve their racial problems will
influence strongly the character and the future directions of
Black student activities, both in the society at large and on
campus.

CAMPUS RACISM, INJUSTICE, AND CONFLICT

Typically, when discussions have arisen concerning racism, conflict, and injustice in American education, liberal, northern, white academics conjure up images of lily-white schools in the south run by incompetent, semi-literate, julep-sipping rednecks, whose chief academic concern is the issue of evolution versus the origins of man as presented in biblical mythology and attended by "nigger-baiting" pranksters, loose and hypocritical "southern belles," and various other psychotics, moral degenerates, racists, and just plain garden variety neanderthals. Although there are, to say the least, some inaccuracies and half-truths in northerners' conceptions of southern education, the implications of the spontaneously negative images of southern white schools that emerge are far more significant than the fact that these images are usually exaggerated and based more upon emotional responses than rational considerations. For such images imply an absolute differentiation between the character, functioning, and quality of academic objectivity in the north as opposed to that exhibited in the south. Such differentiations are not only unjustified, but constitute still another instance of gross northern white self-righteousness, hypocrisy, and the old "we-are-better-to-our-niggers-in-the-north-than-you-are-to-your-niggers-in-the-south" attitude. If all the educational institutions in America were placed on a scale, ranging from the most just and non-racist at one pole, to the most unjust and racist at the opposite pole, there would probably be no discernible relationship between the regional locations of the schools and their posi-

Chapter 8

tions on the continuum. The United States is a thoroughly racist society, and its educational institutions are major perpetrators of its racism. As contributors to the maintenance of the status quo, formal educational institutions in the north differ from those in the south only in that the former are more hypocritical, more covert and subtle, and are productive of psychologically more damaging experiences for those who fall victim to their brand of injustice. As mentioned before, it has become a truism, particularly among Blacks, that anytime a person is south of the arctic circle, he is down south if he happens not to be white. This fact of the Black experience has been greatly reinforced by the discrepancies and contradictions in what formal education in America is portrayed as being and what it actually is.

Racism and injustice: institutionalized components of education in America

The one profession that has contributed more than any other to the maintenance and perpetuation of racism and injustice in America has been the teaching profession. It is the teacher, as an official representative of a secondary societal institution, who first grants legitimacy and validity to the racist attitudes that children—negro and white—learn from their peers, their parents, and from various forms of the mass media during their pre-school years. This reinforcement continues right up through graduate school, although not always deliberately. Indeed, the facts tend to indicate that racism and injustice, as a rule, are so intrinsically interwoven into the total educational experience that the average teacher would find it necessary to make consciously calculated efforts if he would successfully neutralize or minimize racism and injustice in his teaching. But deliberate or not, the results of racist teaching practices are the same.

121

America's curricula: reading, 'riting, 'rithmetic, and racism

Regardless of where or when one attends school in America, he receives, along with legitimate educational experiences, a dose of pure, unadulterated racism. Since the earliest days of this nation's history, students attending its schools have achieved competence in four, not three, "R's": Reading, 'Riting, 'Rithmetic, and Racism. Through overt pronouncement, covert inference, and simple omission, education has made racism—the fourth "R"—the foundation upon which the other three "R's" are based. In doing so, America's school system has not made racism legitimate but has perpetuated and intensified it.

As I have intimated, racism is seldom explicitly taught. But the entire curricula of American schools are thoroughly infested with it. It provides the "set" or framework within which the student learns all his educational skills. But simply because racism is not explicit does not mean that the people who control and determine policy in America's educational institutions are ignorant of its existence and devastating effects upon students. On the contrary, in recent years there has been a raging debate over the issue of racism in educational curricula, particularly as propagated through textbooks. Many educators, Black and white, have repeatedly stated that most textbooks—and therefore, the study plans and other curricula components based upon them—are either totally white-oriented or blatantly racist in content and emphasis. From the standard elementary school *Dick and Jane* reader to the most sophisticated technical tomes used at Cornell, Harvard, and other prestige institutions, textbooks have reflected and reinforced the one-sided white orientation and racist ills of American society. They defame or totally ignore Black people and other minorities. Every minority-group child who attends school in America is de facto insulted and humiliated constantly by materials and books, which nevertheless he must master if he is to "succeed" in school. From their books comes the standard, unbroken message that all the vital figures, heroes, the national giants, are white. It was the white man who built America, turned back its rivers, cleared the forests, built the bridges, created its industry. Even the white woman—Betsy Ross and Molly Pitcher are the exceptions—gets short shrift. The textbook view of America reflects the sick and unrealistic dream of a sick society. And this sickness is passed on to generation after generation by teachers who are, in reality, functioning as "carriers" of America's gravest social disease—racism.

Even a cursory check of most textbooks will reveal that few if any Black adults are mentioned in them. If Blacks are portrayed, they typically are pictured performing menial labor, scraping and bowing before mighty whitey. (The impression students get is that Black people are in America to work, to do as they are told.) Yet known slavers and racists are frequently depicted as heroes and inspirational figures. And if non-whites have somehow managed to defeat or otherwise confound whites, the incidents are omitted, played down, or turned around so as to make whites seem like tragic or sympathetic figures or as the victims of treachery—to wit, General Custer.

Traditional American history textbooks literally have ignored the story of this nation's minorities. Most reflect a strong Anglo-Saxon bias. A great many of the problems that exist in the U.S., particularly in race relations, have been created and have been promulgated not only by misinformation but, what is even worse, by no information at all: censorship by commission and omission. In an article in the *Saturday Review* (September 11, 1965), Elinor Sinette, District School Librarian for the Central and East Harlem Area of New York, wrote as follows:

Publishers have participated in a cultural lobotomy. It is no accident that [negro] history and [negro] identification have been forgotten. Our society has contrived to make the [American negro] a rootless person. The Council for Intercultural Books for Children has been formed to relieve this situation.

Also indicative of the problem is a study that was made a few years ago for the Anti-Defamation League of B'nai B'rith, entitled "The Treatment of Minorities in Secondary School Textbooks." The summary of the finding of the Anti-Defamation League in its chapter "Textbook Treatment of American Negroes" states:

The [Negro's] position in contemporary American society continues to be very largely ignored. There is a tendency to treat racial inequality and attempts at its eradication with complacent generalizations, not hard facts. In most cases, the presentation of the 1954 Supreme Court decision on public school desegregation bypasses any consideration of the underlying principles and of the subsequent ongoing attempts at both compliance and evasion. The achievements of living Negro Americans are mentioned in only a small minority of books. Residential segregation by race is seldom discussed.

Historically, American negroes continue to be portrayed primarily as simple, childlike slaves and as uneducated, bewildered freedmen. Most textbooks do not chronicle the achievements of this people in the years from 1876 to the present. Where attention is given to outstanding negroes in American history, the presentation is insufficient to counterbalance the previously created stereotype of a racially inferior group.

The scientific knowledge underlying sound understanding of the basic similarity and equality of the races of mankind is absent from the great majority of the tertbooks.

With few exceptions, photographs and other illustrations in textbooks continue to portray America as an all-white nation, not as an interracial and increasingly integrated one.

Other general conclusions were:

A majority of the texts still present a largely white, Protestant, Anglo-Saxon view of history and of the current social scene. The nature and problems of minority groups in America are still very largely neglected.

Treatment of the Jews continues to suffer from an overemphasis on their ancient past and on the theme of persecution.

Nazi persecutions of minority groups are inadequately treated.

The Negro's position in contemporary American society is very largely ignored.

Immigrants to the continental United States receive considerable attention in American history and social-problems texts. A more sympathetic portrayal is generally accorded to the post 1880 immigrants from Southern and Eastern Europe than was reported in 1949. Similarly, the history of restrictive legislation is now seldom couched in terms that place an onus on the immigrant. But there is virtually no improvement in textbook treatment of the Asiatic immigrant, who is still shown, in most cases, as a strange, unassimilable outsider presenting a threat to the living standard of native Americans.

Little attention is paid to America's increasingly significant Spanish-speaking immigrant and migrant groups. Little is said in favor of these groups; in several cases, negative stereotypes are still presented. A few textbooks continue to refer to all groups of immigrants as outsiders, but more accounts now reflect the realization that the United States is made better by the richly diversified heritage of its pluralistic citizenry.

Lowell P. Beveridge, Jr., an architect by profession and educational director of the Brooklyn Association for the Study of Negro Life and History, also commented on this situation in an article entitled "Racist Poisons in School Books," which appeared in *Freedomways:*

125

There is in the United States today a national conspiracy to indoctrinate our children with white supremacist propaganda. This conspiracy operates quite openly; it is condoned by most parents' organizations, officially approved by most school boards and indirectly subsidized by federal, state, and local governments. It is able to reach every school child in the country with its insidious, chauvinist literature. I refer to the multi-million dollar textbook publishing industry.

In particular, the social science and history books used in our schools today are, with painfully few exceptions, primers in white supremacy. We should not be surprised that the children of a racist society are taught racism. The reasons for this have been clearly summarized by author John O. Killens: "In order to justify slavery and oppression in our times, the enslavers through their propagandists have to create the illusion that the enslaved people are subhuman and undeserving of human rights and sympathies. The first job is to convince the outside world of the inherent inferiority of the victims of oppression. The second job is to convince the citizens of the country where the enslavers hold forth. And the third job, which is the cruelest of all, is to convince the slaves themselves that they deserve to be the victims. This was the task the propagandists for slavery tackled with alacrity and with great measure of success, the effects of which remain with us even till today, almost a hundred years after the Emancipation Proclamation."

Beveridge ends his article by saying:

As in so many other areas, the white south is the worst offender, but the "liberal north" is also guilty. The campaign for honesty in textbooks must be carried on in the north as well as the south on every possible level: in local elections, in the school boards, in parent and teacher organizations, in the universities, in the classrooms, in professional organizations and in trade unions. While not detracting from the duty and necessity for people of African descent to publish and teach the truth about their own heritage, it is necessary to carry out a parallel campaign against those who would perpetuate lies and distortions about this heritage. THIS IS BASICALLY A POLITICAL PROBLEM [caps interjected].

Thus, in the sick fantasy world of American education, whites are omnipotent, and all minorities—particularly Blacks —are reduced to the status of Orwellian non-people. In the ivy tower, minority group peoples and cultures do not exist until whites "discover" them; Black people came into being in 1619 through the process of spontaneous generation; and peoples having cultures and civilizations in North America long before whites ever left Europe simply melt away as a result of white colonists' friendly efforts to Christianize them and break them of their "savage and barbaric" ways.

If the educational institutions of America are so racist oriented, then, why has no stiff, concerted action been taken to remedy the condition? There are several reasons. First of all, a significant number of educators and academic administrators, as well as large segments of the white public, are opposed to any correction of the problem. An excellent example of part of the reason behind such opposition was evident in California recently when a concerned group of teachers and civic leaders tried to introduce a more balanced and realistic history textbook, *Land of the Free*, into the public school curriculum of that state. The group of educators, outraged parents, and academic officials who opposed use of the new text did so on the grounds that ". . . such a presentation of the Negro in a history textbook would tarnish America's image, rob the majority of America's youth of inspirational heroes, and make white people feel guilty." In short, for these defenders of the status quo, the truth was too painful. It would seem that educators and administrators are having so much difficulty today dealing and communicating truthfully with students because they have not yet reached the point where they can stop lying to themselves.

A second barrier to firm action is that textbook publishers

have catered to the market. And, in a racist society, the people who decide which textbooks are valid are themselves infected with racism. Most publishers have acted in de facto complicity with these racist educators and administrators by bending to the rules of economic expediency and providing them with the slanted, biased books which they favor.

Another factor, connected indirectly with the second point, is that Black people and people from other minority groups have not generally written textbooks. First of all, if these books were honestly written, they, in all likelihood, would not be publishable as textbooks for the economic reason just mentioned. Second, relatively few minority group people have traditionally stayed in college long enough to acquire the expertise needed to write a textbook or co-author one. Moreover, if texts are written or contributed to by minority group persons, these writings and contributions may be more biased in favor of the status quo than the books turned out by white racists. Finally, many publishers, as well as most of the people who decide the relative merits of textbooks, have not yet grown to accept the fact that minority group scholars are competent in areas other than those dealing with racial and cultural problems and intergroup relations.

Now, let us take a closer look at a few of the subjects that make up the general educational curricula in America in order to clarify further this view from the Black perspective.

HISTORY

A widely used college world history text contains within its first chapter two excellent illustrations of the type of subtle and intrinsically racist interpretations of events which have become typical of education in America from the perspective of the Black student.

"In 1492, Christopher Columbus discovered America . . . . and there were people standing on the shore watching him get off the boat . . . . [whom] he called Indians."

Campus racism, injustice, and conflict

"Marco Polo discovered China . . . . and he returned to Europe with spices and riches from civilizations which were obviously hundreds of years old."

Students reading these passages are forced to one of two conclusions. If one is to believe the two scholars who wrote the text, he must assume either that both Columbus and Marco Polo somehow managed to "generate" or "create" the peoples with whom they came into contact during their travels, or that the poeples whom they "discovered" really did not matter since they had not been known by whites to exist prior to the voyages of these white explorers. The first assumption is too ludicrous to warrant further discussion. Not so, however, with the second alternative. For, implicit in the average student's acceptance of the second alternative, is the notion that nothing significant or important occurs in human history until white people come on the scene and make "discoveries." No one would have asserted in March, 1969, when Richard Nixon visited France, that by doing so he had discovered France. All of us realize that there already were people in France, and that to discount their history, their culture, and their existence as irrelevant prior to Nixon's coming would be to do both the French people and human history a rank injustice. But historians' accounts of the first contacts between whites and non-whites are enlightened by no such rationality.

For the Black student, historical interpretations and accounts such as those just examined breed humiliation and smack of effrontery, insult, and degradation. It would be another matter entirely if the examples I have used thus far were isolated or unique. Every course in American history involves the portrayal of some of the people who were active in the founding of the nation as heroes, inspirational figures who by their "saintly" actions and attitudes, set the stage for the development of a "free, just, and democratic society." Indeed, it is part of the social and historical mythology of all surviving modern societies that, for the citizens of each, founding fathers should be perfect and without moral, ethical, or spiritual flaws. But Afro-Americans live in America and arrived here before the English, as sailors with French and Spanish explorers. To portray whites as the faultless, divinely guided founders and sole builders of this nation is nothing but a hoax. But nevertheless, George Washington emerges from the white pages of history books, written by white authors, as a determined fighter for the freedom of all men; Thomas Jefferson is portrayed as a dedicated intellectual and relentless and determined crusader for justice and human dignity; and Abraham Lincoln becomes "The Great Emancipator." Little wonder that Black students gag when they are forced, under penalty of flunking, to regurgitate hypocrisies and outright lies about such men and their commitments to dignity and freedom for all men.

GEORGE WASHINGTON, "THE FATHER OF OUR COUNTRY"

From the time they first enter school, young Americans are bombarded with all manner of myths and fairy tales about George Washington. For grammar school children, "Washington never told a lie." For high schoolers, he is "the defender of justice and human rights." And for college students, he has been likened to Gustavus Vasa "as the deliverer of the nation into a new era of freedom, self-determination, and human dignity"; like Peter The Great, "Washington was the uncorruptible politician and statesman"; and, like Cincinnatus, he is said to have "returned to a simple life, after having achieved the highest honors of the nation, and sought only the approbation of his countrymen by being virtuous beyond peer and always in the service to humanity." Hogwash! George Washington was demonstrably racist and anti-Black, a licentious adventurer who betrayed a life-long friendship by carrying on an illicit relationship with a friend's wife for over forty years.[1]

[1]L. M. Sears, *George Washington,* Thomas Y. Crowell Company, New York, 1932, pp. 10-12.

Campus racism, injustice, and conflict

Washington was a slaver, fathered children by Black slave women (Martha, his wife, never bore him any descendants), and an incorrigible hypocrite. Read some of his own words.

George Washington in a letter to Robert Morris in 1786, on the question of escaped and freed slaves:

I hope that it will not be conceived that it is my wish to hold the unhappy people in slavery. . . . But when slaves who are happy and contented with their present masters are tampered with and freed or seduced to escape . . . by the Quakers of Philadelphia . . . more evils are [produced] than are cured.[2]

George Washington to John Francis Mercer and to one Colonel Spotswood in 1794:

To Mercer:
I never mean to possess another slave by purchase. . . .

To Spotswood:
Were it not that I am against selling slaves as cattle, I would not be possessed of a one in twelve months.[3]

Washington's thoughts on his slaves at Mount Vernon:

. . . [My] slaves are subject to punishment without trial, and are under constant anxiety of being sold; their daughters are desecrated here at Mr. Vernon as "breeding wenches"; all slaves are expected to be honest, truthful, hard-working, and loyal to [me]. [Their] thieving of foods and goods are habitual and [they] evade work by pretended illness. They constantly plague [me] with alleged promises of freedom.[4]

George Washington, entry in his personal diary in 1795:

[2]Howard Swiggett, *The Great Man,* Doubleday & Co., Garden City, New York, 1953, pp. 439-440.
[3]Swiggett, *op. cit.,* p. 440.
[4]Swiggett, *op. cit.,* pp. 441-442.

I had resolved that I would never obtain another slave by purchase; but this resolution I fear I must break.[5]

A letter from Edward Pushton in 1797 to which Washington made no reply:

The hypocritical bawd who preaches chastity, yet lives by the violation of it is not more truely disgusting, than one of your slaveholding gentry bellowing in favor of democracy. Man does not readily perceive defects in what he has been accustomed to venerate; hence it is that you have escaped those animadiversions which your slave proprietorship has long merited. For seven years, you bravely fought the battles of your country, and contributed greatly to the establishment of her liberties—yet you are a slave holder! You are a firm believer too, and your letters and speeches are replete with pious reflections on divine being, providence, etc.—Yet you are a slave holder! Oh! Washington, ages to come will read with astonishment that the man who was foremost to wrench the rights of [America] from the tyrannical grasp of Britain was among the last to relinquish his hold on the poor and defenseless negroes.

In the name of justice what can induce you to tarnish your own well-earned celebrity and to impair the fair features of [American] liberty with so foul and incredible a blot? Your slaves . . . are worth about fifteen to twenty thousand pounds. Are you sure, sir, that your unwillingness to free your slaves is not the result of your own attitudes towards their human status and from some lurking pecuniary considerations? If this be the case, then there are those who believe that there is no flesh left in your heart; and present reputation, future fame, and all that is estimable among virtues, are for a few pieces of paltry yellow dirt and stubbornness against reason being renounced.[6]

[5]Sears, *op. cit.*, p. 489.
[6]Sears, *op. cit.*, p. 489.

All this information, and much more, is easily available to any novice student, but not in his textbooks. When he runs across such data, doing research for assigned class projects or papers, he is forced either to conclude that his teachers, his texts, and most of the other information on Washington which he had been exposed to is wrong, or that Washington, in fact, never did tell a serious lie that, in fact, he was perfect, and that therefore his attitudes and actions toward Black slaves were right and consistent with American ideals of freedom and justice. Black students invariably conclude that they have been victimized, and degraded, for their entire existence has been marked by victimization and degradation. They have been taught to honor and revere a man who believed in the innate inferiority of Black people and who enslaved, brutalized and undoubtedly was responsible, at least indirectly, for the deaths of some of them.

As for Thomas Jefferson, the same holds true.

THOMAS JEFFERSON

Although somewhat less "saintly" a textbook figure than Washington, Jefferson was equally as racist, if not more so. For, Jefferson intellectualized his racist attitudes and rationalized the fact that he was a slave holder. Like Washington, he fathered children by Black slave women, even though he, too, was married and had a white wife living on his plantation. Few history textbooks mention these facts. Nor do they state that while Jefferson was "coining" the Declaration of Independence, a slave—a Black man, one of those things that whites don't want their daughters to marry, who was his personal servant at the time—was sitting at his very feet. But this obvious contradiction never phased Jefferson, so deep seated was his commitment to racism. His position never seems to have wavered.[7]

[7]All following references are from J. P. Foley, *The Jeffersonian Encyclopedia,* Funk and Wagnalls Company, New York, London, 1900, pp. 11-14.

Thomas Jefferson to Jared Sparks on legislation to forcibly emancipate the slaves, 1824:

Actual property has been lawfully vested in the form of [slaves] and who can lawfully take it from the possessors?

Jefferson on anti-fugitive slave regulations in Florida, 1791:

We have perceived with great satisfaction notification of the orders . . . that [slaves] are no longer permitted to present themselves as free persons in the Province of Florida. In the same spirit and principles of justice and friendship, we trust that you [the Governor of Quesada] will allow recovery of [slaves] who have hitherto taken refuge within the political bounds of your government.

Jefferson on the "improvement" of Black People, 1782:

The improvement of [Blacks] in body and mind in the first instance of their mixture with white blood has been observed by everyone and this proves that their inferiority is not the effect of their condition of life. It is obvious to all that [Blacks] are not equal in body or mind to whites although this is difficult to affirm.

Jefferson on slaves and music, 1782:

In music they are more gifted than whites with accurate ears for tune and time, and they have been found capable of imagining a small "catch" [a rudimentary form of the banjo and precursor to the modern guitar], but it is doubtful that they have the [mental] capacities to . . . compose more extensive melodies and scores or more complicated harmony.

Jefferson on racial amalgamation, 1814:

The [Blacks'] amalgamation with the other colors produces a degradation to which no lover of his country, no lover of the excellence of human character can innocently consent.

Jefferson on the emancipation of his slaves, 1782:

The unfortunate differences in color and faculties [are] powerful obstacles to the emancipation of these peoples. Many advocates of emancipation, while they wish to vindicate human liberty, are also anxious to preserve its dignity and beauty. The slave, if set free, might wish [to mix] with whites . . . and in doing so stain even the . . . blood of his master. So if freed, he must be removed beyond the reach of mixture.

For Jefferson, Black people were eternally to be inferior to whites. He could not see himself as moving in any way to relieve the legal compulsory subservience of Blacks, although he often remarked that ". . . after my lifetime, others must move to undo the centuries of wrong done by whites to [negroes]." However, it was not until Abraham Lincoln's time, almost a century later, that any efforts were made by national officials to free Blacks. But even here, the facts of emancipation differ noticeably from textbook accounts concerning the principles and ethics that motivated Lincoln to free the slaves. In short, Lincoln was, as were Jefferson and Washington, a self-admitted racist.

ABRAHAM LINCOLN

If necessary, I will free all of the slaves, some of the slaves, or none of the slaves; whatever is necessary to save the union.

Whereas I am aware of the injustices of slavery, the public sentiment is such that [Blacks] repulse whites by their very presence, and if the two races must abide within the confines of a single nation, then, for my part, whites must be in a superior position and [Blacks] must of necessity be inferior.

From these and other utterances, it becomes clear that Lincoln did not sign the two pieces of emancipation legislation out of a fundamental commitment to freedom and justice for all. He did so out of a desire to serve the interest of northern white industrialists and other enemies of the plantation-based agrarian south. But so elaborate a web of myth has been spun around Lincoln by historians that he has become a symbol of civil rights and the champion of Black people. If one wants to locate the Black school in a strange city, his best bet will be to hail a taxi and ask the driver to take him to Lincoln School; if one wants to visit a Black recreational facility, he simply looks for Lincoln Park or Lincoln Pool or the Lincoln Gymnasium.

Like Jefferson, Lincoln advocated the deportation of all Blacks from America, even though many had fought in the war for independence from England and in the Civil War against the south and had worked in building the country virtually without pay for almost three-hundred years prior to emancipation. Like both Jefferson and Washington, Lincoln was convinced of both the innate inferiority of Black people and the superiority of whites. Unlike Jefferson and Washington, however, there is no evidence that he ever exploited Black slave women or owned slaves.

How do Black students respond to such disclosures? Chagrined and angry, they realize that they have been taught to respect and idolize men who regarded their forebears as inferior. To continue to revere them would be to sanction their racism. To forsake them would be to divest themselves of the pitifully few "heroes" the textbook writers have permitted them. For Blacks have been written out of American history almost completely and the William Lloyd Garrisons and John Browns who fought and campaigned for human dignity and justice have been portrayed as fanatics or fools.

But the history books are by no means the sole offenders. Other disciplines are just as much to blame.

136

Campus racism, injustice, and conflict

In most sociology textbooks, the words "Black" and
"Afro-American" do not appear. This omission is not unique,
for such designations do not appear in most course textbooks.
If Black students want to read sociological material about
themselves or their people, they must turn to the index and
look up the word "negro." In three sociology textbooks currently in wide use the word "negro" is indexed as follows:

(1) Negro, p. 314
    see also:
        crime
        delinquency
        illegitimacy
        illiteracy
        deviate family structures

(2) Negro, p. 219
    see also:
        racial problems
        race riots

(3) Negro, p. 112
    see also:
        etiquette
        illegitimacy
        illiteracy
        "passing"
        prejudice
        race riots

If a Black student wants to gain an understanding of his
own people free of the inherent biases of white authors, he
will be hard pressed to find appropriate and up-to-date materials. He will come away from the average sociology text
with the unmistakable impression that Black communities

are little more than havens for sexual deviates, addicts, illit-
erates, and various other types of social, moral, and ethical
degenerates. The fact that such texts usually patronizingly
assert that these conditions result from a long history of white
racism does not soften the subtle but nevertheless devastating
impact such descriptions create. And while few reputable
sociologists today would venture that Blacks are innately
inferior as a race, many of them nonetheless continue in their
writings and the slant of their lectures to perpetuate racism.

A specific case of institutionalized racism in sociology
involves the widely read and publicized "Moynihan Report."
The author of the "Moynihan Report," Daniel P. Moynihan,
is presently a member of President Nixon's cabinet and heads
the forces whose chief concern is finding solutions to the
nation's urban problems. In commenting on the Moynihan
Report, Andrew Billingsley, in his *Black Families in White
America*, writes:

Moynihan and his staff examined the 1960 national census data
and found that nearly a quarter of all negro families were headed
by females, and that nearly a quarter of all negro babies that year
were born out of wedlock. These are facts which negroes, social
workers, and students of the negro family have been aware of and
concerned about for some time. These statistics alarmed Mr.
Moynihan. He concluded, quite incorrectly, that the negro family
in this country is falling apart and failing to prepare negro children
to make their way in the world. According to this view, the negro
community is being destroyed at least as much by its own family
structure as by the indifferent and often hostile society around it.
While his own data showed quite the contrary, Moynihan concluded that "At the heart of the deterioration of the fabric of negro
society is the deterioration of the negro family. It is the fundamental
source of the weakness of the negro community at the present time."[1]

[1]Daniel P. Moynihan, *The Negro Family: The Case for National
Action,* Washington, D.C.: U.S. Department of Labor, Office of Planning
and Research, March, 1965, p. 1.

Campus racism, injustice, and conflict

Because the 25 per cent of negro families headed by females was so much higher than the proportion of white families headed by females, Moynihan paid very little attention to the fact that 75 per cent of negro families met his criteria of stability. There are a number of methodological and substantive problems with the Moynihan report.[2] A major distortion was his singling out instability in the negro family as the causal factor for the difficulties negroes face in the white society. It is quite the other way round. But coming just at the time the nation was trying to find a single cause of the Watts riots, Moynihan's thesis struck a responsive chord in the collective American breast. ". . . At the center of the tangle of pathology," he concluded,

> is the weakness of the family structure. Once or twice removed, it will be found to be the principal source of most of the aberrant, inadequate, or antisocial behavior that did not establish, but now serves to perpetuate the cycle of poverty and deprivation.

He could come to such faulty and inverse conclusions in part because he had no theoretical framework to guide him in the analysis of his statistical data, and in part because his data were limited.

Another serious shortcoming of the whole report was the tendency, common among liberal social scientists, to compare negroes with whites on standardized objective measures which have been demonstrated to have meaning only in the white, European subculture. Many statistical studies which compare negroes and whites fall into the almost inevitable position of characterizing the negro group as deviant. If all a study can describe about negro family life is what it simultaneously describes about white families, it cannot tell us very much about negro family life. Moynihan compounded this error, however, by his failure to take into account two very important aspects of the negro experience: social class and social caste.

[2]Lee Rainwater and William L. Yancey, *The Moynihan Report and The Politics of Controversy.*

Simple white-negro comparisons on almost any set of standardized variables will necessarily produce distortions, for they ignore the important dimension of social class. The white sample will contain large numbers of middle and upper income families and the negro sample will be dominated by low income families. Using statistics for the same year, Moynihan found that 25 per cent of negro families were broken. Lee Rainwater has shown that if one considers only negro families with family incomes of $3,000 or above, this proportion dropped from 25 per cent to 7 per cent, while for negroes earning less than $3,000, it rose to 36 per cent.[3] But while income level explains a great deal of the original racial differential, it does not explain it all. For at all income levels, the rate of broken families is higher among negroes. Thus among white families earning $3,000 or under, the rate is 22 per cent—considerably less than the 36 per cent for negro families. And among white families earning $3,000 and over, it drops to 3 per cent, less than half the negro rate.

This brings us, then, to the second major variable overlooked by Moynihan, despite his own analysis of this factor elsewhere in his report. We refer to the importance to the negro experience in America of the caste-like barriers which exclude negro families from so many of the resources of the society. Even when the income *levels* are similar for the white and the negro samples, the two groups are not comparable. For we know that even in the low income category of under $3,000, the mean income for white families falls considerably toward the top of that range, while the mean income of negro families is considerably lower. A white family with an income of $2,750 and a negro family with an income of $1,500 are both under $3,000 and both undoubtedly lower class, but they

[3]Additional critiques of the Moynihan Report are William Ryan, *The Nation,* November 22, 1965; Benjamin F. Payton, *Christianity and Crisis,* December 13, 1965; Herbert Gans, *Commonweal,* October 15, 1965; Hylan Lewis, Agenda Paper, White House Planning Conference (unpublished); and Laura Carper, *Dissent,* March-April, 1966. Each of these papers is reprinted in Rainwater and Yancey, *op. cit.*

do not have the same resources and options available to them. Even if two groups of white and negro families were matched with exactly the same income, education, and occupation, they would still not be comparable. For the negro group must reflect its experience with the caste barrier as well as its distinctive history, both of which set the conditions for growing up black in white America. Thus, white-negro comparative studies may be very important for certain purposes, but they are wholly inadequate for understanding processes of causation and other dynamics of negro family life, particularly if they are conducted without a general theoretical framework.

The low income negro family faces three insidious problems. One is poverty, the other is prejudice, and the third is historical subjugation in his own country because of his race. The low income white family faces only one of these problems, and in this respect is better off than even the middle class negro family—contrary to the implications of the Moynihan report. For the middle class negro makes considerably less money than the middle class white, and in addition, must face the color bar in ways unknown to the experience of his white counterpart. However powerful the variable of social class, it does not obliterate and, indeed, was not invented to account for the racial factor.

But those very social scientists who insist that Moynihan's only sin was that he ignored social class are themselves guilty of ignoring even more powerful definers of the conditions facing negro families in this country. Negro family life in America is circumscribed by a complex set of social conditions which shape the family in various ways. The Moynihan report is only a more recent and popular example of studies which do not take cognizance of these complexities.

POLITICAL SCIENCE

In political science classes, Black students are told by their teachers and read in their textbooks that America is a democracy wherein all persons who are born or naturalized citizens have certain unalienable rights. They likewise learn that the United States government and the Constitution stand behind every citizen who seeks redress of his just grievances and that America is a country governed by laws and not by oligarchies, cliques, or dictatorship.

Yet Black people are de facto defined as "second class citizens," a category not recognized by the Constitution. On analyzing the leadership of congress, however, one begins to understand how the catagory is maintained. Admitted racists control the congress, and it is upon these men that Blacks must depend for justice and reform.

Everett Jordan, N.C., Senate Rules Chairman; William Colmer, Miss., House Rules Chariman; Carl Perkins, Ky., House Education and Labor Chairman; Richard Russell, Ga., Senate Appropriations Committee Chairman; John Stennis, Miss., Chairman Senate Armed Forces Committee; William Fulbright, Ark., Chairman Foreign Relations Committee; John McClellan, Ark., Chairman Government Operations Committee, Senate; Wilbur Mills, Ark., Chairman House Ways and Means Committee; Allen Ellender, La., Chairman Senate Agriculture Committee; James O. Eastland, Miss., Chairman Senate Judiciary Committee.

That these men occupy positions of power and leadership in government today is ludicrous. It is roughly analogous to making Willie "the actor" Sutton the night watchman at a bank, or putting foxes in charge of a chicken coop, or leaving a lettuce field in charge of a pack of rabbits. Yet in their political science and history classes, Black students are told that the south lost the war! The south is, in fact, more powerful and influential in the U.S. government today than ever before. And Black students realize this. To teach them that America is a democratic society is to teach them that Black people are irrelevant and not equal to whites.

Campus racism, injustice, and conflict

LITERATURE

Few schools or colleges in America offer literature courses that include the works of Black writers. The average Black student today is infinitely more aware of the works of white writers, many of whose writings reflect racist attitudes, than they are of Black writers. Consequently, Black students are denied the opportunity to study about the Black experience in America. Their Black heritage is denied them.

LANGUAGES

Like literature, languages taught in America's schools have traditionally been of white European origin, and, until very recently, not even the most advanced universities offered any courses in Black African languages or dialects.

MUSIC

Music appreciation courses in America's schools still revolve around the "classical compositions." Although Black people have produced the only truly American music, it is the music of another age, another place, and another people that Blacks must learn to "appreciate" if they are to pass a music appreciation course. Could it be that in today's modern American educational system there are those who feel, as did Jefferson, that Black people do not have the intellectual capacity to create quality music, and therefore that their creations must be inferior and of poor quality?

PHILOSOPHY

The average Black student (the average white student, for that matter) cannot name a single Black philosopher from any era in human history. White philosophy, much of it racist, is all he encounters during his educational career.

143

Like Black musicians, writers, and philosophers, Black painters and other creative artists are virtually ignored in America's colleges.

The dreary, humiliating listing could go on and on, but extending the list would not even begin to scratch the surface of the problems faced by Black students. Even extra-curricular activities offer small relief, for these are often as racist infested as are the courses and instructors, and usually the racism is a lot less subtle than the classroom-textbook variety.

The Black athlete: the shame and the glory

With the emergence of racially mixed athletic teams, the Black athlete found himself in refreshingly new, but sometimes brutally dehumanizing, educational and athletic environs. Not infrequently, the Black athlete approaches life and athletic participation on the predominantly white college campus with the anticipation of a child in a carnival arcade. He was in the past, as he is today, usually somewhat unsure of his abilities—social, athletic, educational, and otherwise. He often feels during his first few weeks on campus that perhaps he has misjudged his athletic potential; perhaps he has listened too long and too intensely to the cheers and praise of high school rooters in his home town; perhaps he has overrated his ability and will be doomed to "ride the pines" for three or four long years. Questions about education also plague him. Many Black athletes come to predominantly white schools under "special adjustments," usually instituted on their behalf by the coach at the college. Will he be able to make the grade academically—even with the help of the tutors promised him by the Athletic Department, and with the "mickey mouse" courses prescribed for him by his coach —"at least until he finds his study legs"? Will he be able to write acceptable papers and keep up with all his other course requirements? And what about campus social life? When not practicing or studying, how will he spend his time? Will he fall naturally into the normal campus social whirl? Will he want to?

The question of the Black athlete's ability is usually the first to be resolved. For it was his ability that brought him to the attention of the coaches in the first place. Before official practice even starts at most college campuses, the coaches of the various sports always make certain that their newly recruited freshmen and transfer athletes have access to the necessary equipment to carry on "informal work-outs on their own." Under the watchful, searching eyes of the coaches, the Black athlete goes through his paces in football drills, pick-up basketball games, and batting and fielding drills in baseball —and sometimes over the course of an academic year, he does all three. For, the Black athlete in the predominantly white school was and is, first, foremost, and sometimes only, an athletic commodity. He is constantly reminded of this one fact, sometimes subtly and informally, at other times harshly and overtly, but at all times unequivocally. The Black athlete is expected to "sleep, eat, and drink" athletics. His basketball, football, or baseball (depending upon the season) is to be his closest companion, his best friend, and in a very real sense, the sole symbol of his concern.

The Black athlete generally fares well compared to incoming white athletes at the white dominated college. The cards are somewhat stacked in his favor, however, because few Black high school athletes get what are typically classified as second and third string athletic grants-in-aid. One simply does not find Black athletes on "full-rides" at predominantly white schools riding the bench or playing second or third string. Second and third string athletic grants-in-aid are generally reserved for white athletes. And whites never encounter the pressure that Black athletes face. For everyone expects the Black athlete to excel, and if he does not, he has let down the coach, the school, and the entire "negro" race.

He is suspected of "goldbricking," breaking training, lacking concern for his teammates.

Educationally, the Black athlete traditionally has done little better at white schools than he would have done at a negro college. And as much as white racist coaches and athletic directors at white-dominated colleges would like to attribute this apparent intellectual deficiency to inherent racial shortcomings, such is simply not the case. As a matter of fact, the reasons why Black athletes at white schools are herded into "mickey mouse" courses can be traced to the racist attitudes of the coaching staffs at white schools. Insofar as many white coaches and athletic directors are concerned, the world does not need Black doctors, chemists, dentists, mathematicians, computer operators, or biologists. Moreover, such lofty academic goals might interfere with the athletes' playing career and the colleges' financial investment in them would be jeopardized. Besides, how many Black doctors, chemists, dentists, and biologists, does the average white coach know? Not many, if any at all; and so, according to his racist way of thinking, Black people simply do not possess the necessary gray matter to go on to such professions. So, the coaches think—when they consider the matter at all—why put the "boy" under pressures that will prove too great a strain for him? Instead, install him in a four-year academic program that will qualify him for a B.S. degree, but a B.S. degree in basketweaving, car washing, or janitorial skills. But not many accredited schools offer degrees in such areas, and still fewer jobs are available for persons possessing such credentials. As a result, proportionately few Black athletes graduate from predominantly white schools within the four-year time period covered by their span of collegiate eligibility. In fact, many never graduate at all. Having neither the personal funds to finish school after their athletic eligibility has expired nor the necessary academic background to qualify for aid on scholastic grounds, the Black athlete simply falls by the wayside, or he goes, with his press clippings, trophies, plaques, and his four years of irrelevant education, and applies for a job in a factory or on an assembly line. If he is extremely lucky, he gets a job, or he is able to sign on with some professional athletic team—and this new step opens up a whole new chamber of horrors for the Black athlete. But, by and large most Black athletes simply return to the slums of America to face again humiliations and defeats they have suffered all their lives.

Perhaps the cruelest cut awaiting the Black athlete on the white-dominated campus arises from the dismal and repressive social conditions he encounters, particularly the restrictions—formal and informal—involving participation in fraternity and sorority life, school dances, parties, and the dispensing of student body funds.

Officially, the Black athlete on the white campus is a duly registered member of the academic community and therefore is subject to all the rights and responsibilities thereof. This is his "official" status. Unofficially, and more to the point, vast areas of college life are closed to him. With a few notable exceptions, the Black athlete at a white college never becomes famous enough, athletically or otherwise, to warrant his being accepted by a fraternity. In areas where integrated white schools and Black schools exist in fairly close proximity, it is not unusual to find Black athletes joining fraternities at the Black schools because they are excluded from the white-dominated fraternities on their own campuses. Many of their white teammates may, and usually do, belong to these racist organizations. I can recall clearly how I resented white teammates of mine who belonged to organizations and participated in activities that were detrimental to my social well-being and still had the nerve to talk to me about "team spirit" on Saturday. But I soon found out as most Black athletes at white schools do, that white teammates can call you and every other Black person they know niggers, coons, and jiggaboos six days a week and then jump at you with calls for team spirit on Saturday afternoons. I had several fights with white teammates who "jokingly," they said, called me nigger and coon. I "walked into" numerous conversations between whites in the locker room discussing "jiggaboos" and "night-fighters." And not all these whites were players at the school. Some were coaches, team managers, and trainers. One never adjusts to these things. He either fights, and risks being branded a trouble-maker, or he ignores them. During my collegiate athletic days, I did both.

Fraternities, then, having their origins primarily in the south and maintaining what may be construed as distinctively southern characteristics, are the exclusive domains of whites on most big college campuses. They ease the social adjustment of the incoming white student, but also serve as convenient drawing cards for coaches attempting to recruit white athletes for their schools. As a matter of fact, the first sign of racism the Black athlete encounters comes during the recruitment stage—before he is even enrolled in school.

The first stage in the recruitment process involves inviting a prospective athlete to campus to look it over and get a feel for it. A day is generally selected when some special event is scheduled—homecoming, or a basketball game. Both Black and white athletes are invited and shown around the campus, all the while being sold on the advantages of attending this institution rather than another. This "togetherness" comes to a screeching halt, however, when the time for the inevitable socializing arrives. After all, the coach would not want his new recruit to feel that at "Jock Strap U." things were all business and no play. What generally happens at this point is that the prospective athletes are separated—by the coaches —along racial lines. The prospective white athletes are assigned to white athletes already enrolled at the school and usually participating at the varsity level in the sport for which the incoming athlete is being recruited. Inevitably, some of these campus stars are members of fraternities and, through their membership, are able to line up dates for the recruits, put on parties and dances for them, and generally give them a feel for the social life of the institution. The Black recruits also get a realistic feel for the social life and college spirit of the campus—but from the Black perspective. As was the case with the white prospective athletes, the Black recruits are escorted by presently enrolled Black athletes. There are some significant differences, however.

First of all, the incoming Black athlete is not always escorted by another person engaged in the same sport for which the recruit is being sought. For not all athletic fields on white campuses were integrated at the same time. As a result, a Black being recruited for basketball may be escorted about the campus by a football player or track man. Second, the Black escorts usually do not have access to fraternities and sororities, so there are no parties, dances, and other "after-game" activities for the Black recruit. And woe to the Black who goes, uninvited, to a party at a white fraternity or sorority, even though all his white teammates and their guests may be there. Instead, the coach generally will give the Black recruit's escort ten or fifteen dollars and bid them farewell until some specified time the following day. And since there are usually few, if any, Black females on these campuses— they typically are not six-feet-eight-inches tall and know nothing about dribbling basketballs, kicking footballs, or swatting baseballs—time hangs heavily on the Black recruit. For the fortunate, there sometimes may be ghettos not too distant from the campus or tourist spots such as Juarez, Mexico, which is practically adjacent to the campus of the University of Texas at El Paso. For the less fortunate, as was true in my case, you spend the evening having dinner in a second-rate restaurant, go to a third-rate movie, and then return to a dull, dreary room in some isolated corner of the campus to "talk sports."

How does a white coach justify this double standard of treatment? Usually, the same set of rationalizations pop up.

Some coaches feel that "negroes feel more comfortable with their own." Others say that to mix athletes at social events would alienate the white players and their dates. Still others reply that things have always been done this way or simply "cop out" by pretending ignorance. Regardless of the excuse, the shattering effect of the experience cannot be eased.

A related, but somewhat different, problem involves choice of dating partners on a white campus. If there is any aspect of the informal social codes on white college campuses that applies most emphatically and almost singularly to Black males, it is the code that covers interracial dating. And the warning "Don't be caught even talking to a white girl, much less dating one," has been driven solidly home to the Black athlete. This dictum is prescribed by white coaches and enforced by white teammates who often report to coaches any incidents of interracial dating between Black athletes and white females. White team members also will belittle and slander white females who date Blacks. For most white men believe that any white female who even talks to a Black male, much less dating him, must be carrying on some sort of lewd affair with him or is obsessed with the alleged sexual prowess of Black men in general.

Outside the athletic arena, then, the life of the Black athlete is lonely, monotonous, and unrewarding, even before he enrolls at a white school. He may be a hero on the field or on the court, but in street clothes and even in the locker room he resumes his status as "just another nigger." Once on campus, the Black athlete finds that he does, in fact, become part of the big team; and he is an important part. As the head basketball coach at San Jose State College, Dan Glines, once emphatically stated, "Without the Black athlete, you don't have a chance in this game. You don't draw fans, and you don't win." But the Black athlete also finds that his equals are not his white teammates but the basketballs, baseballs, jockey straps, and other forms of property and equipment—all of which, like him, are important and vital to sports. And like a piece of equipment, the Black athlete is used. The old cliché about "You give us your athletic ability, we give you a free education" is one of the biggest lies ever concocted by the white sports establishment to hoodwink Black people. There is no such thing as a "free" ride. The Black athlete pays dearly with his blood, sweat, tears, and, ultimately, with some portion of his manhood for the indoctrination he receives at a white educational institution. Moreover, white athletic establishments on various college campuses frequently fail to honor even the most rudimentary obligations entailed in their half of the agreement. Few schools, it would seem, provide the tutors so often promised to Black athletes prior to their enrollment. Typically, the coach, rather than providing tutors, simply obtains copies of tests which are then distributed among the Black athletes. (This also happens upon occasion with white athletes, but not very frequently. Sometimes it is not even necessary for the coach to secure a test for a failing white athlete, because the athlete may have already secured the test, from the back files at his fraternity house.) And, if he is injured, or if he fails to live up to the expectations of the coach who recruited him, the Black athlete may be required to work at various campus jobs to "help balance things out."

Black athletes are constantly being reminded that whites regard them solely as a piece of property. As indicated, in the social and educational areas of college life, the Black athlete is expected to function at a sub-human level. In athletics, he is expected to be super-human. Whites expect him to run faster, jump higher, dribble better, pass fancier, and play longer than any of his white teammates. The Black halfback in football who has only average speed does not play. The Black basketball player who cannot jump, dribble, or otherwise distinguish himself as a "super-nigger" does not play. He is expected to be tireless. If he slows up, it is because he

151

is not in shape or "lazy." He is always supposed to go at top speed, and if he doesn't, he has let the entire negro race down. He can afford no mistakes, no temporary slip into mediocrity.

A practice common on most white-dominated college campuses is the technique of "stacking" Black players in one position or another in order to limit the number who actually make the team. Only the top Black high school athletes, as we mentioned, are offered grants-in-aid to the big-name schools and they are under intense public pressure to accept these offers. These conditions, added to the fact that white players do not have to be and are not expected to be as good as Black athletes, mean that theoretically most of the positions on predominantly white college athletic teams could, in fact, be manned by Black players. But the coaches neatly avoid this predicament by "stacking" Black players at one position or another—such as halfback or end in football, or center or guard in basketball—and letting them fight it out among themselves for the positions on the team that are open to them. The results are usually the same. A few Blacks make the team, usually in first-string positions. Other Blacks with athletic ability far and above that of many of the whites who make the team are summarily dropped or told that they can stay on the team but without full financial support or with no support at all.

Other techniques for maintaining the quota system on predominantly white teams are equally as simple and as effective. At most white-dominated schools, certain positions are reserved outright for whites. Most familiar of this racist maneuver is the reservation whites hold on the position of quarterback. Racist coaches really believe that Blacks lack the brains and know-how to handle that position. The tremendous burden of remembering plays, assignments, and generally running things on the field is "too much for the coon's mustard-seed brain to handle," as one college team trainer remarked to another during the course of a football game at a mid-western university in the fall of 1966. Less common but equally as racist is the belief of many white coaches that Black men cannot play offensive guard on big-time football teams because of "genetically based intellectual deficiencies" that prevent them from remembering pulling and blocking assignments.

If white coaches, white athletes, and white students are so repulsed by Black athletes, why is he recruited? We have already alluded to the answer. One only need read the minutes of the congressional hearings on the dispute between the National Collegiate Athletic Association and the Amateur Athletic Union to understand that amateur athletics in America is big business. By my calculations, the dispute between the N.C.A.A. and the A.A.U. centers about the control of ten million dollars presently held in banks and investment capital by the A.A.U. The N.C.A.A. maintains that a sizeable proportion of these funds derives from the efforts of college athletes affiliated with the N.C.A.A. and that, therefore, the N.C.A.A. should have a cut of the booty. In addition, individual schools fare handsomely from amateur athletics. Athletic receipts build libraries and laboratories. A player such as O. J. Simpson or Lew Alcindor, during the course of his college eligibility, is worth approximately three million dollars in gate receipts and television rights to his school. Every white coach who recruits a Black athlete hopes that he has uncovered a potential O. J. Simpson or Lew Alcindor, because it means money and prestige for the school, and money and prestige for him. And what does the Black athlete receive in return? Most often, with few exceptions, he receives his walking papers as soon as his eligibility is up. He becomes another has-been who never really was.

Then why do Black athletes elect to go to white schools if they encounter nothing but mistreatment from the time they are recruited until they remove their cleats or sneakers for the last time? The answers to this question are as varied as the dreams and hopes of the many Black athletes who yearly leave urban and rural slums to attend predominantly white schools. Perhaps a more pertinent question would be, Why do they stay? Black athletes stay on racist white college campuses because of a driving obsession to prove themselves and because in the Black community itself severe stigma falls upon the Black athlete who goes to a big name school and "fails to make the grade." If he fails academically, he is ridiculed; but if he quits, he is despised. For he has voluntarily turned down "the chance that his parents didn't have." He has failed those who had faith in him. He has added validity to the contention held by white folks that Black people are lazy, dumb, and quit when the going gets rough. In essence, then, he is despised because he has failed to prove himself to whites. He has failed to demonstrate that he can take it. The Black athlete himself may feel guilty about the thought of quitting. But what he and many other Blacks fail to realize is that, quit or stick, he can never prove himself in the eyes of white racists—not as a man, not even as a human being. From the perspective of the average white American, he is, and will always be, a nigger. From their point of view, the only difference between the Black man shining shoes in the ghetto and the champion Black sprinter is that the shoe shine man is a nigger, whereas the sprinter is a fast nigger. But both are niggers.

The Black athlete on the white-dominated college campus, then, usually is exploited, abused, dehumanized, and then cast aside like a worn-out basketball. His lot from that point is not really different from that of any other Afro-American. His life becomes an endless round of insults, humiliations, and all other manner of degrading experiences. The coach will no longer call a racist landlord and request that he rent to the former Black athlete because he was a "good negro." Few white coaches work to get Black athletes respectable summer jobs while they are eligible for sports; small chance they will do anything after the athletes' eligibility has expired. The athlete is finally and desperately on his own. Then, and only then, do most realize the degree to which they have been exploited for four long years. Consequently, some simply give up on society and join the armed forces. Others attempt to cling to the one commodity that they had been able to peddle, however cheaply—their athletic ability. These pathetic, brooding, Black figures can be seen playing in hunch games and city-league games in any college town at all times of the year.

Of course, there is always the periodic return to the old college campus to play against the new recruits and relive some of the old excitement—if they are invited. The ex-athletes seldom tell new Black recruits the truth about the "big team." They avoid having to answer questions about why they, themselves, stayed on for four years. They want the recruits to look on them as heroes, Black men who proved themselves on the athletic fields, where each man is rated according to his courage, his ability, and his winning record. They avoid questions and the truth because they are desperately trying to preserve whatever masculine qualities they have left and are clinging to the delusion that in some way the past four years of their lives had been everything that they had wanted them to be. For them, the future looks dismal and hostile, and the present is a farce. The only phase of their lives that they can control is their past, and this only through delusion, self-deceit, and lying. Although the philosophy of separatism is predominant to a large extent on campuses today, racist attitudes and practices in athletics still weigh very heavily on Black athletes who must work closely with whites.

Racism and injustice in curricular and extra-curricular activities, were a prime cause of campus confrontations, adding to the traditional four "R's" of education a fifth—Rebellion. But it takes two sides to force a confrontation, and upon analysis the educational institutions of America themselves emerge as major fomenters and perpetuators of campus conflict.

The educational institution as a perpetuator of campus conflict

The structural character of the educational institution—particularly the colleges and universities—and the relationships between its various functionaries and constituencies predispose it to be unresponsive to rapid, radical change in crisis situations. In its lack of capacity for such change, the educational institution aids in the creation of the conditions necessary for the perpetuation and intensification of conflict and confrontation, particularly where racial issues are involved.

On predominantly white college campuses, the elements which predispose such institutions to perpetuate conflict are essentially six: (1) the structural component of a two-semester or three-quarter academic year cycle, with long stretches of time—especially during the spring—wherein there are no vacations or breaks of any significant duration; (2) the recruitment of significant, but insufficient, numbers of minority group students; (3) the relationships between the university and the military and economic institutions of the society; (4) a significant degree of dependence upon alumni for financial aid as well as for certain administrative and trustee duties; (5) amorphous and overlapping authority and responsibility between faculty and administration; and, (6) the existence of highly factionalized student bodies, having within their ranks students of diverse and often conflicting political persuasions.

The university is, essentially, a service organization made up of professionals and experts. Its primary public is its student body. As functionaries in service organizations, the professional teachers and research and administrative experts who control college campuses are reluctant to share either authority or power with students. To many faculty members and administrators on today's college campuses, to allow students—any students—to have a voice in determining what faculty members will be granted tenure; what courses will be offered; or what student admissions, grading, and financial-aid policies will be is roughly analogous to turning an asylum over to the inmates.

This tendency of service organizations to fight radical changes and shifts in power and authority relationships is intensified, in the case of a university, when students begin to organize into mutual-aid associations, such as Black student organizations. There exists a contradiction and the seed of inherent conflict in the fact that university officials have recognized such mutual-aid associations and incorporated them into the formal structure of the institution. For in doing so, they have conceded the legitimacy of student claims for some power and say in university policy and practices without being willing actually to grant them any. Actually, the recognition of Black student organizations by educational institutions has been motivated largely by a desire to co-opt dissident students and their movement into the traditional university structure and thereby to mute their demands. It has not worked. Rather than co-opting the dissidents, university officials, faculties, and other academic officials have whetted student demands and precipitated the inevitable confrontation. The lines thus have been drawn between two legitimate and mutually recognized organizations—one, the university, a service organization; the other, the Black student organization, a mutual aid organization. One is made up of professionals and experts; the other one is made up of the professionals' primary public constituency. One organization, the university, is committed to the maintenance of traditional academic standards and student performance and behavior, whereas the other, the Black student organization, is determined to reform radically all aspects of college and university life.

APRIL 1969: CONFRONTATION AT CORNELL, A CASE STUDY

From the testimony and opinions of observers of the events of April, 1969, at Cornell University, three key points have emerged:

1. The rigidity of existing institutional arrangements preclude change except under extreme conditions, despite academicians' claims of rationality and adaptability.

2. Fundamental structural change will occur only after institutions such as Cornell suffer the shock of broader and deeper violence.

3. That the crisis experience is so unsettling to all officially connected with the institution that from it emerges an incredible amount of effort aimed at rationalizing, explaining, and ordering events in an attempt to restructure future institutional functioning toward change.

Although there were few unusual things about the Cornell confrontation, the appearance of guns in student hands, while an inevitable dynamic of confrontation, represented an escalation of student activism with major ramifications for Cornell and the nation at large. Accordingly, the Cornell case is worth considering in some detail.

Student activism at Cornell

Cornell's April confrontation began on the eve of the university's 104th anniversary. During its first one-hundred years, Cornell, like most American universities, was untroubled by

Chapter 9

Confrontation at Cornell, a case study

political activism. Although a land-grant university, Cornell was converted, under the beneficent guidance of Ezra Cornell, to a private institution. Despite its Ivy League aura and the relative isolation of the campus in south central New York, Cornell is a mixed university, drawing many types and classes of student to its colleges and schools.

Up to World War II, student life at Cornell followed the rah-rah and fun and games pattern that prevailed at most Ivy League schools. After the war, the student base was broadened by the influx of ex-G.Is. During the McCarthy period, according to an article by Susan Brownmiller,[1] what political life there was at Cornell died and, indeed, the creative impulse of the student body was seriously damaged. In the late 1950's, some activism arose over sexual issues, culminating in a riot in 1958 over the right of students to attend mixed parties without chaperons. Enshrined by Richard Farina in his book, *Been Down So Long It Looks Like Up To Me*, the demonstration produced little change other than shifting the responsibility for student conduct from the president to the faculty. The loosening of controls over student behavior continued to move sluggishly, and it was not until 1962 that senior undergraduate women were released from curfew; indeed, it was not until 1968 that the faculty abandoned the doctrine of *in loco parentis* concerning personal student behavior.

Political activism at Cornell did not begin until the early 1960's. Two broad social issues—the Viet Nam war and race relations—were the generating factors. The initial impetus came from Berkeley, but it seemed to have lost much of its force by the time it had reached the Ithaca campus. The main result was the organization of a group known as Students for Education (SFE), which lived a short but exciting two months before being washed away by the February, 1965, Vietnam escalation. SFE gave rise to study commissions and some tepid changes, such as the conversion of the campus

[1] "Up From Science," *Esquire*, March, 1969.

bookstore into a real bookstore rather than merely a purveyor of required texts, the creation of an on-campus coffee house, and some feeble and well-controlled changes in the grading system.

As the Vietnam war escalated, Cornell students organized anti-war protests, including a major confrontation during an ROTC review in Cornell's cavernous Barton Hall, later the center of action during the 1969 events. In succeeding years, the university was confronted on various war-related issues concerned with military recruitment and the right to solicit pledges to burn draft cards.

Throughout this period, the organizational center of student activism became the Students for a Democratic Society (SDS). The lineal descendant of earlier Cornell leftist experiments, SDS at Cornell developed much as SDS developed on most other campuses—as anti-organizational, anti-leadership, and committed to spontaneous, consensus decision-making procedures. Although organizationally amorphous, SDS had been relatively effective because of its capacity to mobilize student (and some faculty) energies.

The race issue

Cornell has always had a few negroes on its campus since the early 1900's, and many of them have made notable records for themselves. But largely because of its rural isolation and its essential WASPishness, the number of Blacks at Cornell has always been negligible. Into the early 1960's, the number of Blacks attending the university from outside the United States far exceeded the number of Afro-Americans.

Until the Supreme Court decision of 1954 outlawing school segregation, Cornell's atmosphere, like that of most American universities, was almost unashamedly racist. Many fraternities and sororities forbade membership to non-caucasians. After 1954, the atmosphere changed, and liberal pressures began to work against the restrictive membership clauses of the "Greeks." These pressures later focused on the elimination of discrimination in off-campus housing.

Until the mid-1960's, these pressures came primarily from Cornell's white liberals and radicals. As the civil rights movement took form, Cornellians, first individually and then as groups, found themselves involved. Several Cornell students went to Fayette County, Tennessee, to work on getting Black people registered to vote.

Two conditions reduced white involvement in civil rights activities in 1965. First, the development of Black consciousness, the belief that Blacks should lead and control the movement, led to the exclusion or alienation of white civil rights supporters. Second, the escalation of the Vietnam war provided an alternate cause for liberal and radical whites.

Meanwhile, more significant changes were approaching at Cornell, aided by an increase in the number of Afro-American students on campus. Embodied in outreach and support programs, the Committee on Special Educational Projects (COSEP) located and recruited Black students and provided them with financial and other support. COSEP's successes, although small, nevertheless succeeded in bringing 240 Black students to Cornell by September, 1968. The increasing numbers of Black students produced considerable strain in the university, which began to manifest itself publicly in 1967-68 over three issues.

Black separatism came to the fore when a Black girl, living in the girls' dorms, ran into some difficulties with her dormmates. The girl was referred to Cornell's clinic for psychiatric assistance, but not responding as expected, she finally was ordered to leave school. Her refusal precipitated a crisis, which expressed itself in demands for separate Black housing so that Blacks could develop along their own lines without the pressures of living in a strange, often hostile environment. Despite misgivings, arrangements were made to establish. several Black co-ops.

Academic freedom, as an issue, arose in an economics class, taught by a visiting professor, in which Black students and others became convinced that the instructor's approach was racist. After complaining to every relevant agency of the university and being put off time after time, the Blacks confronted the professor with a demand that they be permitted to read a statement before the class. When he insisted on reading it first, and the Blacks rejected his request, he dismissed the class. The Blacks thereupon took over the Economics Department, holding the department's chairman in his office.

The assassination of Martin Luther King occurred on the same day as the Economics Department sit-in. The two events shook the university community. Several fires were set, clearly the work of an arsonist, and the Blacks utilized the memorial service for Dr. King to attack the university administration and America's whites in general.

The events of 1967-68 indicated that the base for Black organization had been established. While not yet coherently organized, the Afro-American Society was working out its internal problems.

Confrontation 1969: the immediate background

In response to the events of the 1968 spring term, the university moved to set up an Afro-American studies program. A committee was formed, composed of nine faculty and administration members and eight Black students, which met during the summer and fall. During the second week of December, the Black student members revolted against what they thought were stalling tactics by the committee. They demanded total control of the program and refused to participate any longer in the committee's work. That same week, six members of the Afro-American Society forced three whites to leave their offices in a university building on Wait Avenue, a building which the administration had promised would be used for the Afro-American studies program. A reporter for the *Cornell Daily Sun*, who refused to turn over a film, was roughed up during the affair. Meanwhile, covert negotiations between the Black students and the administration continued over the students' demand for an autonomous Black studies program. Although the Black students set several deadlines, little progress toward meeting their demands was made, and the Blacks saw this as another expression of the administration's unwillingness to consider their demands seriously. One week before the Christmas recess, Black students at Cornell decided to stage demonstrations to indicate their displeasure. The campus was treated to two days of Black marches paced by bongo drums. The President's office was entered by Black students armed with water pistols. Some white students were removed from several tables in the student union, which then were designated "Black tables" and reserved for Blacks. Carrying hundreds of books from the library shelves to the checkout counters, Black students abandoned them as "irrelevant." They also marched on the clinic and demanded to be treated by a Black physician. Despite their sometimes humorous aspects, these demonstrations had an ugly and threatening undertone, which left most whites tense. Faculty and administration responses were hostile, and the process of finding scapegoats got underway. But the protest had been convincing enough to move the administration toward implementing the Black studies program. Not all Black demands were met, but a Black director was tentatively chosen and compromises were worked out on making the program a degree-granting one and insuring that credit would be given by the university for the courses offered. Thus, the Black students saw their demonstrations as part of a political program that was necessary to help them gain a meaningful education at Cornell.

In January, six students involved in the pre-Christmas

demonstrations were charged before the Student-Faculty Conduct Board, and the decision handed down provided one of the two sparks that touched off the 1969 confrontation. The disciplinary issues were complicated when Black students intervened during a conference on apartheid sponsored by Cornell's Center for International Studies. The South African symposium, with 25 speakers, of whom only three were Black, was out of touch with its audience, which was composed preponderantly of Afro-Americans, Black Africans, and SDS supporters. Questioning from the floor gave way to more physical approaches. At a meeting on the second evening of the conference, the Blacks turned out en masse to challenge Cornell President James Perkins on university investments in South Africa. As Perkins addressed himself to this issue, one Black student grabbed Perkins by his collar and pulled him from the podium. The shaken President withdrew, and the session ended inconclusively. Campus reaction was hostile to the Blacks, despite increasing sentiment that Cornell should liquidate its South African investments.

Meanwhile, the Afro-American Society charged that the demonstrations for which the six Black students had been called to account were political acts for which the organization alone should be held responsible. Prosecuting a few members, the charge added, could only be regarded as victimization. Accordingly, the six refused to appear before the Conduct Board. They were threatened with suspension and when they still failed to appear, were sent letters notifying them of the penalty they faced if they persisted. Finally, in April, an obscure clause was discovered in the university constitution permitting the Conduct Board to take action without the students being present. On April 18, the Board reprimanded three of the Blacks, dismissed charges against two others, and dropped the charge against the other student who had left the university.

Throughout the late winter and spring, campus groups

had been enunciating principles to support or oppose the issues involved. For the Conduct Board (and implicitly for the faculty and much of the student body), the main question at issue was: Is the university a single community? If this is *a* community, must all "citizens" adhere to its rules? The Blacks not only challenged the idea of *a* community, but put forward the principle that no man should be judged except by a jury of his peers. The Blacks attacked the legitimacy of the Board, contending that it was an extralegal adjunct of the campus community and owed its existence to racist sentiment. To partly justify their position, the Afro-Americans pointed out that there was no Black representation on the Board. A second conflict of principle arose over the issue of how personal, in contrast to political, acts could be judged. Appropriate university bodies argued that individuals rather than organizations had to be held responsible for their acts; organizations could not be tried before the Conduct Board. The position of the Blacks was not only that their acts were political, but that such actions had to be treated as organizational acts rather than as violations of university conduct codes. The Blacks also argued that the university was not only the aggrieved party, but the judge and jury as well; principles of Anglo-Saxon justice required that the injured party not be judge and jury. The Afro-American Society suggested that "arbitration" on the industrial relations model might resolve the problem.

In addition to the disciplinary issue, a number of other questions were unsettling the university. During their seizure of the Wait Avenue building, the Blacks had insisted that their demands for an Afro-American studies program were "non-negotiable." Nevertheless, extensive discussions continued (frequently through intermediaries), although many faculty members took the term "non-negotiable" at face value and interpreted the position of the Blacks as intransigent and obdurate. Nor had the issue of Black separatism gone down

165

well with much of the university community. After the December demonstrations, as mentioned earlier, several tables in the student union had been clearly demarcated as Black territory. Blacks moved around the campus in groups and gave up fraternizing with whites. None of this sat well with most of the faculty and students.

While the focus of attention centered on the Blacks, a host of other issues were affecting large numbers of white students. SDS had made demands that the university provide housing not only for students, but for the Ithaca community. Arguing that the university had thrown the burden of housing upon the community, SDS insisted that the university provide low-cost housing units for underprivileged people in Ithaca. Although centered outside the university, this issue generated considerable support in faculty and student circles: a network of housing organizations was created to bring pressures for a university commitment in this area. A second issue burgeoned over the impending departure of several well-known historians and humanities professors. For many years the humanities area has been weak at Cornell and neglected by the administration. The situation became a mobilizing element for many Arts and Sciences students. Still other grievances existed for graduate assistants over financial support and over Cornell's South African investments. And, in mid-April, just before the confrontation, a popular sociology professor, one of the first winners of a teaching award, was refused tenure because of his weak publication record. This created additional tension.

These issues, plus others, created an atmosphere of tension that had threatened to come to a crisis as early as on Wednesday, March 12, when the university faculty was scheduled to meet. The faculty adopted a resolution supporting the integrity of the adjudicatory machinery, despite the dissatisfaction and complaints of the Black students. The crisis continued to simmer.

Confrontation 1969: the seizure of the student union

At 3:00 a.m. on the morning of Friday, April 18, the very day the Student-Faculty Board was to meet to decide the case of the December six, a burning cross was thrown on the porch of the Black girls' co-operative by party or parties unknown. Responding to a call, the campus safety patrol reached the co-op and put out the fire. Details concerning the precise actions of the campus safety patrol at the scene of the cross-burning are not fully clear, but apparently all seven officers covering the incident withdrew, ostensibly on other business, leaving the co-op unprotected. Although a guard was assigned later, in answer to Black demands, the Blacks' confidence in the campus security forces was severely shaken. It did not help when campus officials, while strongly deploring the incident, referred to it as a "thoughtless prank." To the Blacks, the symbolism of the event was as powerful as if someone had burned a *Star of David* in front of a Jewish fraternity. Had such an action occurred, the Blacks reasoned, all of the powers of the university would have been brought to bear, and the cries of outrage would have been heard around the land. But the somewhat cavalier attitude that the university took toward the incident seemed but another reflection of the institutional racism about which the Blacks had been indicting the university for so many months.

Nor had earlier incidents—Black girls being called "niggers" by white boys in cruising cars—create an atmosphere of interracial friendship. As word of the cross-burning circulated among the Blacks, they assembled at the co-op to decide what action was necessary to protect Black co-eds on campus. This issue was to be paramount in the seizure of Willard Straight Hall. The Blacks felt that the time had come to demonstrate to the campus their unwillingness to tolerate any more racism.

Another factor contributing to the Blacks' decision to seize

Willard Straight Hall, the student union, was that Parents' Weekend had begun, and the dramatic opportunity that situation held out was clear. How significant a role this consideration played in the seizure is hard to say, but its strategic implications were obvious. Specific demands temporarily were shelved. The Blacks were intent on an expressive and demonstrative warning to the campus to "get off their backs." The original intent was to seize the building for one day only and then surrender it peacefully.

At 6:00 a.m. on Saturday, April 19, the Blacks marched into Willard Straight, calmly ordered service personnel preparing for the day's activities to leave, locked up the building, and expelled from the loft, containing guest rooms, a number of parents visiting for the weekend.

News of the seizure soon spread throughout the campus; by 8:00 a.m., it was common knowledge that the university was on the brink of another confrontation. The presence of so many parents on campus irritated many students, particularly the more conservative, many of them fraternity men and residents of lily-white houses. One of these fraternities, Delta Upsilon, is sometimes called the "jock house," because so many of its members are athletes. It is also one of the most WASPish houses on campus; there are no negro members. Around 9:00 a.m., about fifteen to twenty DU members tried to enter Straight Hall, and some eight or nine did push their way in before a host of SDS members sealed off the entrance once again. During the pushing and shoving inside and outside the building, three whites and one Black were injured, although none seriously. After finally expelling the DU men, the Blacks announced that any other attempts at entry would be countered by increased force. SDS members, arrayed outside in sympathy with the Blacks, rejected a proposal to seize another building but set up a picket line around Willard Straight to show their support.

The DU attack was interpreted in various ways, but from the viewpoint of the Blacks, it represented an attempt by the

Confrontation at Cornell, a case study

university to oust them from the building. Although the campus patrol was ostensibly guarding the building to prevent entry, the fact that a number of people had gained admittance indicated to the Blacks that the campus guards simply were looking the other way. Thus, the Blacks interpreted the foray as a thinly disguised administration attempt to oust them, instead of what it probably was—a spontaneous, self-organized attempt by fraternity boys. On their part, the DU men insisted that they had entered the building to discuss the situation with Black athletes inside, and that there was no intent to recapture the building. (There was no evidence, however, that any Black athletes were involved in the seizure of the student union.) The DU men claimed that they went in empty-handed; the Blacks insisted that they came in with clubs.

The incident touched off a spate of rumors. Throughout the day reports persisted that armed vigilante groups were preparing to mount an attack on Straight Hall. Inside the building, telephone messages kept arriving confirming the reports. By Saturday afternoon, according to the testimony of the Black occupiers and administrators in telephone contact with them, the Blacks were in a state of considerable tension, and finally decided to bring in guns to protect themselves. Thirteen rifles and two shotguns were smuggled into the building and some crude spears were fashioned by those inside. Although the night passed quietly, the rumors and alarms continued. By Sunday morning, Cornell administrators, confronted by a deteriorating situation, decided that the occupation had to be ended regardless of the implications or consequences.

That the occupation of Straight Hall was a precipitous, largely unpremeditated action probably triggered by the cross-burning is borne out by two facts: (1) the length of time it took the Blacks to formulate their demands; and (2) the relatively innocuous nature of the demands. By Saturday afternoon, three demands had emerged from Willard Straight, one of which was subsequently withdrawn. The first demand stipulated that the reprimands handed out to the December demonstrators be withdrawn; the second called for a full investigation and report to the Afro-American Society of the cross-burning incident. That the Blacks would resort to such extreme measures to back up such inoffensive demands indicates their state of tension. The Blacks' torment and distress did not register except with those who were in direct contact with them. Amid these circumstances, the administration formulated a six-point agreement to end the Straight occupation, including a commitment to call a full faculty meeting to recommend that the reprimands be rescinded.

The agreement ended the Straight occupation, but the Blacks were determined to demonstrate to Cornell whites that they would no longer meekly accept racism on campus. Accordingly, despite pressure from administrators that they exit submissively, with guns under cover, the Blacks proceeded to file out of the building with weapons brandished. Photographers on the spot had a field day. It soon became convenient for the shocked white majority of the university to look upon the incident as a new escalation in student activism, for this was the first time on any campus that dissident students had taken up guns.

Confrontation 1969: into the crucible

The spectacle of armed students marching across their campus was too much for the overwhelming majority of the Cornell faculty although most had accepted the cross-burning with relative calm, classified it as a "prank." Unable to grasp the feelings of the Blacks, the immediate reaction on Monday, April 21, was one of bitter hostility to any compromise or accommodation to Black demands. Antagonism focused on the six-point agreement reached between the administration and the Blacks. Some forty members of the faculty, largely in the Government and History Departments, signed a statement to the effect that they would resign from the university if the reprimands were voided at the faculty meeting.

Tension increased during the day as opposition mounted within the faculty. What the reaction of the Blacks would be to a refusal to withdraw the reprimands was unclear, but the fear of a shoot-out was in everyone's mind. Amid these tense circumstances, President Perkins convened a convocation in Barton Hall just before the university faculty meeting. Some 10,000 students, faculty, and staff assembled to hear a tepid twenty-minute statement by the President that left issues more unresolved than before. Presidential leadership was never asserted.

Instead, in a strained atmosphere saturated with the hostility of the Government and History Departments, the faculty assembled at 4:00 p.m. The meeting began with a report by Dean of the Faculty, Robert Miller, who began to explain the events after first introducing a formal motion calling for withdrawal of the reprimands. The Dean's assessment was that the protection of human life took priority over the maintenance of adjudicatory machinery, an approach that was rejected by the majority of the faculty, which voted a substitute motion sustaining the adjudicatory machinery and taking no action on rescinding the reprimands. During more than four hours of intricate parliamentary maneuvering, the hostility of most of the faculty remained implacable. Despite an earlier issuance of a proclamation of limited emergency, a decree that anyone carrying guns on university property would be suspended summarily, or that disruptive demonstrations would lead to immediate suspension, President Perkins derived little political capital from the meeting.

It was clear that no consensus was possible at the meeting. The faculty was badly split, with an overwhelming majority opposed to accepting the Black students' demands and an obdurate, vocal minority supporting the Blacks or concerned about the consequences of refusing to accede to the demands. In this context, President Perkins introduced a resolution, which achieved a minimal consensus, calling for discussions between the Faculty Council and the Afro-American Society and for another full faculty meeting.

Dean Miller now tendered his resignation, stating that by refusing to vote on his motion, the faculty was repudiating his estimate of the situation. The standing ovation given the Dean underlined the faculty's dilemma. While respecting him, the majority firmly refused to make concessions to what they regarded as threats of occupation or armed coercion. The meeting ended at 8:15, and the faculty departed for long-delayed dinners. Sunday brought no new developments and an SDS meeting of 2,500 on Monday evening yielded inconclusive results as SDS waited for the Blacks to determine their course of action.

By Tuesday morning, the campus was approaching near chaos. Many classes did not meet, and in those that did, discussions involving the confrontation superseded all formal class work. The university leadership, seeking desperately to shore up a deteriorating situation, called the deans of the colleges into session and proposed meetings of college faculties and the beginning of broad-based discussions at all levels. The intent was to channel rampant, free-floating, anxious dialogue into constructive discussions geared to finding solutions to problems. In the vacuum created by the administration's willingness to make concessions and an obdurate faculty, the administration sought to continue discussions in order to forestall shooting.

By noon, an ephemeral organization called "The Concerned Faculty," consisting largely of elements supporting the Blacks, convened for several hours. Urged to action by members of the Afro-American Society, "The Concerned Faculty" was unable to formulate any clearer decisions than had been generated during the faculty meeting the preceding evening. Twenty-six of those attending agreed to seize a building if necessary, while some sixty-odd faculty members announced their willingness to strike.

Confrontation at Cornell, a case study

The scene of action shifted, however, to meetings of the faculties of the various colleges. Here, the beginning of an apparent change in campus opinion set in, as the colleges of Arts and Sciences and Home Economics recommended to the over-all faculty that all standing actions taken against accused Blacks be nullified. At 7:00 p.m., the Faculty Council called another meeting of the faculty for Wednesday noon and, at the same time, urged that the reprimands be withdrawn. Despite the shift in opinion, several faculties were primarily oriented to the maintenance of business as usual.

By late Tuesday afternoon, student opinion on campus began crystallizing around a call by SDS and the Inter-Fraternity Council for a teach-in at Barton Hall, the largest building on campus. Thousands of students moved to the hall early in the evening, prompted by the belief that another confrontation—or possible gun battle—had to be avoided and that rational discussion and evaluation of the situation was the only hope of restoring calm to the troubled school. During the evening, a consensus emerged concerning the necessity for Cornell students to remain in the building to pressure the Cornell faculty, which was scheduled to meet the next day, April 23. SDS speakers proposed that the students in the hall declare that they had seized the building and challenge President Perkins' new regulation prohibiting such actions; only a handful objected. Later in the evening, President Perkins granted permission for the demonstration to continue, defining it as a teach-in rather than as a seizure, as the students had described it. Thousands made preparations to sleep-in; soon sandwiches and drinks were being dispersed among the mass of students.

As the evening of Tuesday, April 22 wore on, students began organizing their pressure groups according to the colleges they attended. Around the fringes of the hall, dozens of individual meetings involving hundreds of students were held. At 3:00 a.m. Wednesday the meetings were still going on, involving now not only groups from the different colleges, but also various *ad hoc* committees on the press to consider the position of the *Sun*, the university's student-operated newspaper, and one large group of biology students who were attempting to deal with the problem of a professor who refused to cancel a quiz scheduled for the next day. The mood was still tense, but hopeful. Student sentiment obviously had shifted dramatically to the Blacks, although it was less clear if the shift involved acceptance of the Blacks' cause on its merits or if it reflected fear of violence.

Wednesday, April 23, the sit-inners were wakened by a banjo ensemble, and soon the speech-making began again. Although Barton Hall remained the nerve center of events, hundreds of meetings and convocations were being held elsewhere on campus, and faculty members were being approached by students lobbying for their votes at the scheduled noon faculty meeting.

This meeting, chaired by Provost Dale Corson, indicated that a clear shift had occurred within the faculty, despite the hard line taken by government and history faculty members. A motion to nullify was replaced by a second motion, which not only called for nullification but also for restructuring the university. The substitute was introduced by Professor Clinton Rossiter, who had, on Monday, April 21, been a signer of the statement threatening mass resignations if the reprimands were lifted. Biology professor William Keaton explained how a large and representative delegation of his students in Barton Hall had asked him to change his vote, not because he was being coerced, but because they wanted him to have faith in them. But the probable major reason for the shift was expressed by Nobel physicist, Hans Bethe, who said that since the "middle" was behind SDS, it was necessary for the faculty to reverse itself to split the middle away from the Left. The resolution calling for nullification and restructuring the university carried by a voice vote, probably on the order of three or four to one. The faculty now accepted a resolution by philosopher Max Black informing the students "We hear you. . . ."

The overwhelming majority of the faculty members then moved to Barton Hall, where they received a standing ovation. The faculty action emphasized to the students their influence on the decision-making process; from this point, emphasis shifted to the second part of the Rossiter resolution on restructuring the university.

As the faculty arrived, Eric Evans, Vice-President of the Afro-American Society, was speaking. President Perkins arrived and came to the podium where, according to Evans, he put his arm around him, smiled in a fatherly way, and said, "Sit down, I want to talk." Reflecting the new mood, Evans refused to surrender the microphone, and was hilariously cheered by the throng of students still in the hall when he informed them of the exchange. While Perkins fidgeted uncomfortably on the floor with the students and faculty, Evans continued a leisurely review of events leading up to the Willard Straight seizure. When he had finished, he surrendered his place to Perkins, who spoke, seemingly to show everyone he had not deserted the campus, and then was followed by a succession of other speakers. The Barton Hall gathering seemed to have been the catharsis that relieved the tensions of the past five days. By 5:00 p.m., the teach-in had ended, and Cornell entered upon a new course ostensibly dedicated to restructuring.

Roots of the next confrontation

The period immediately following the Barton Hall episode was marked by organizational "withdrawal" symptoms. The most nihilistic withdrawal involved SDS, which either refused, or lacked the capacity, to come to grips with the absence of organization and the need for leadership. The faculty, by their actions on Wednesday, April 23, had gradually changed its negative stance, but the early scars that the Willard Straight incident had left were too deep to heal quickly and the faculty seemed unlikely to be able to function as an effective corporate body. The Afro-Americans retreated into themselves to assess the situation and try to decide how to relate to the college community under the new circumstances. Among other things, this involved renaming themselves The Black Liberation Front and trying to develop a new set of norms for themselves.

In addition, administration officials and traditionally apathetic students also withdrew. The administration was in a state of shock; all that emerged from Day Hall, the administration building, were generalized statements, reinforcing previous statements about guns and disruptive demonstrations. Beyond that, Day Hall demonstrated no capacity to provide any guidance or direction. The students lapsed into an amorphous body. Once the Wednesday catharsis took hold, they lost capacity and motivation to act coherently.

In these circumstances, the tendency was to revert to the traditional, though weakened, institutional structure. Students and faculty turned to colleges and departments, that is, to traditional and more manageable social units. The cooling-off process began. It was not that everyone began to behave exactly as in the past, rather that the reniggerization of the students had begun. In this process, students once again came into direct face-to-face relations with their teachers, to whom they had always given deference. There was a return to the traditional superordinate-subordinate relations that had existed prior to April 19. As early as Thursday afternoon, it was evident that students had begun falling into the old student roles.

By the following Thursday, one week later, reniggerization was complete; although committees and departments continued to meet, no more confrontations between students and faculty developed. Student statements became more qualified and less concrete and hard line. Faculty statements became more rigid and attentions turned once again to traditional issues such as teaching vs. research and academic freedom.

The cooling-out mechanism became focused upon a "constituent assembly," which grew out of an *ad hoc* Barton Hall committee of students (and some faculty) called the Barton Hall Community. Following instructions from the Faculty Council, a faculty committee was organized to deal with the Barton Hall Community and recommend future procedures. These became embodied in a proposed constituent assembly, which received faculty blessing only after a lengthy discussion which focused on a concern about SDS taking over the proposed assembly and radicalizing it beyond the control of the faculty. The faculty's hesitance reflected its concern with protecting its own rights; not only did various speakers raise questions about what the constituent assembly might do, but Professor Hans Bethe obtained faculty commitment to form a committee to delineate faculty rights. The constituent assembly was finally "legalized" by faculty action several weeks after the week of the confrontation with the understanding that it would make recommendations only to existing centers of authority—trustees, faculty, administration. It provides for a 367-member body, of which 116 delegates (32%) will be faculty, 38 (10%) will be graduate students, and 97 (26%), undergraduates, with the remaining delegates representing various other groups and strata at Cornell. The Ford Foundation has given Cornell a $25,000 grant to support the constituent assembly.

The constituent assembly is hardly likely to be a radical body because the unit of representation will be the academic department. Because departments will elect representatives, those delegates will be primarily concerned with existing structural interests. In addition, the fact that students will be representing constituencies normally subordinate to the faculty will structure relationships along traditional lines. Student delegates will be reluctant to challenge professors from their own departments and thus invite reprisals. The assembly probably will operate with all the deliberateness that characterizes faculty proceedings. And, the summer afforded a long cooling-off period.

It does not necessarily follow that the faculty will be unwilling to change at all. But what changes are made will be oriented toward maintaining the existing structure and co-opting into it such pressure groups as may arise or re-emerge. The major emphasis now is alleviating pressure, not solving problems. The only thing the faculty seems to have learned from the experience is that students should be represented in various university organizations. A more fundamental commitment to change is not evident.

Onset of the next confrontation

If the situation we have just outlined persists, obviously new and more serious disturbances will occur. A number of other features of campus life also add to the factors which hold the promise of creating further pressures within the university. The first of these features is the cycle of the academic year. The fact that much campus action takes place in the Spring is neither a function of weather nor of "the sap rising"; rather, it is a feature of the curious sociological character of the university as a social system. At the end of each academic year, a host of student leaders are turned out. This precludes the possibility of these experienced leaders picking up their organizing and mobilization activities where they left off. At the beginning of the new year, a new cohort of students has to be socialized into how the system operates. Typically the fall semester or quarter is the period during which these new leaders establish themselves. As a result of the long Summer recess, substantial changes occur in interpersonal relationships; when people return, they have to reorganize themselves and start learning about those they dealt with in the past and acquaint themselves with the orientations of the new students. Another feature of the academic cycle is that the fall semester is broken up by two long holidays, whereas the spring semester is interrupted but once, at Easter. This leaves a fairly long period without the breaks that permit critical situations to cool off.

Another indication of further trouble is that the pressure in the system, coming primarily from the Blacks, will continue, for two reasons. First, Blacks will continue to be recruited for Cornell in gradually increasing numbers, but not heavily enough to preclude the formation of a tightly-knit, cohesive Black community on campus. Second, the new Blacks will reflect more militant origins than the present crop of Black students. Due to greater recruitment efforts, new Black students will be coming more from hard-core ghettos than the present generation of predominantly middle-class Blacks. They will be more alienated by the university climate, because the educational process will be even less relevant to their experience than to the present generation of Black students. Moreover, ghetto Blacks will be less patient with the deliberate character of university decision-making, bureaucracy, and the interminable wait for change.

It is, perhaps, worth a short digression here to examine why so few Black students at Cornell have created such enormous pressures (and we limit ourselves to the Cornell experience here, although some of this analysis is appropriate to the situation at other universities). While much of the phenomenon can be traced to the sense of guilt currently being experienced in liberal academic circles, much more depends upon the internal dynamics of the social situation on campus—a relatively small number of Blacks in an overwhelmingly white university. All students must adapt to problems that accompany living in large residential universities. Thrown together and living through a host of curricular and extra-curricular problems, they manage to adapt in several ways. In fraternities and sororities, pressures are managed through heavy doses of ritual and brotherhood. In co-ops, the same thing is accomplished by emphasizing social harmony and the advantages of voluntary action rather than compulsion. Dormitories push out to the campus. Students are not called on to interact intensively in the dormitory, but function external to their living situation in classroom, clubs, and other campus organizations.

As the number of Blacks increased at Cornell, they experienced the usual problems that Blacks confront in a white environment. Moreover, the present generation of Black Cornellians entered the university as Black Power ideology began to spread and take hold in Black communities across the nation. Both these factors drew them closer together and strengthened the bond among them. Instances of harassment and discrimination spread rapidly among them and intensified their solidarity. They began to act against what they regarded as an oppressive situation with a strength belied by their meager force. If more Blacks had been involved, this cohesiveness and unity would have been difficult, if not impossible, to attain.

Still another factor pointing toward future confrontations issues from the discrepancies between students' hope for change and the structural inabilities of universities to make significant internal changes, especially in the educational process. Cornell's basic educational system will continue without significant structural change. This will create serious problems, in view of student demands for restructuring. At the same time, the social conditions contributing to this demand remain unresolved: poverty, discrimination, racism, pollution of the environment, and the war in Vietnam continue and are interpreted, probably correctly, as worsening. Students hold high hopes for university reform. Many are naïve in thinking that reform will occur by itself. Probably about a third of Cornell's students believe that something tangible will come out of Barton Hall. If little or nothing emerges, they will become increasingly frustrated and unruly.

These factors predispose the next confrontation. The

specific issue which triggers it can come from any irritant—recruitment by corporations (which most universities will not or cannot eliminate because of majority white student demand, alumni (financial) pressure, and other considerations), pressures for open admission of Blacks and other underprivileged minority groups—unless the university can adapt to change, which seems unlikely.

Conclusion

The Cornell confrontation and its repercussions provide a number of important lessons concerning student activism in the United States:

1. The race issue remains highly potent. The Cornell experience illustrates the dilemma of liberal whites with respect to Blacks in America. Despite Black separatism, closure, and hostility to whites, adult white liberals appear to be shedding their guilt over the plight of Blacks and other minorities in America, which indicates that further progress will be slow if not stymied altogether, especially since this shedding of guilt is not coupled with a greater understanding of the Black experience. At Cornell, however, the support of white students for the Black demonstrators was strong and encouraging. From a strong initial hostility to the display of arms, Cornell's white students developed empathy and sympathy for the condition of the Black students on campus. Their response may well counter the apparent indifference of their elders.

2. Cooperation between the Blacks and Students for a Democratic Society at Cornell indicates that a new period of joint effort by Blacks and whites may be dawning. Prior to the confrontation, the Blacks had gone their own way, and despite SDS interest in cooperative endeavors, there had been little working together. The fact that Cornell's Afro-Americans felt the need for SDS support, and that SDS was willing to follow their general lead, created a condition in which

some organizational cooperation was possible. This does not mean that strong attachments will develop, for there are fundamental differences in approaches.

3. Even though thousands of Cornell students were involved in the confrontation, the revolution is not yet at hand. For one thing, sitting-in *en masse* is a passive act that does not require the high levels of commitment necessary to reform a university. In addition, on such a mass basis, many are carried along with the crowd. In Barton Hall students with close-cropped hair and wearing fraternity jackets could be overheard gleefully commenting, "If only my parents could see me now" or, "We've grabbed Barton Hall." Thus, a sudden, unusual outpouring of energy must not be confused with a long-term sense of commitment or dedication to change.

4. Following the Barton Hall sit-in, it became clear that student power had reached a new level and faced new problems. Until the April confrontation, student power was an abstract issue. The recognition that Cornell's faculty could no longer rule the university without student consensus has created a new set of conditions which require that programs be devised and implemented to give meaning to the slogan "Student Power." For the moment, no such programs exist; an intellectual and ideological vacuum seems to have enveloped the campus.

5. One unusual element in the Cornell situation, unlike previous confrontations at other universities, was the respective positions of faculty and administration. In most other recent student demonstrations, the faculty has been to the left of the administration, with the latter acting to preserve the *status quo*. At Cornell, the administration had a much more realistic estimate of developing pressures and was prepared to make concessions in order to avoid a show-down. Even when the majority of the faculty shifted positions between the Monday and Wednesday meetings, a hard core still opposed relinquishing any power to the students. They

regarded any kind of capitulation as an erosion of academic freedom. Although there were no formal challenges to academic freedom and only a handful of threatening comments were made by a few extremists, hard-line faculty members interpreted threats to non-academic faculty prerogatives (e.g., control over student discipline) as threats to their academic independence.

6. One aspect of the Cornell experience in particular illustrates that the contentions of Blacks that institutional racism exists in academia are accurate. This is reflected in the fears that both liberal and conservative white faculty members exhibited for the safety of themselves and their families when diffuse threats were made against them or specific names were mentioned. Several faculty members felt sufficiently menaced to move their families to local motels. Terror was loose at the university and they were unable to perform their normal functions. Yet these same faculty members were unable to grasp the idea that Blacks inside Willard Straight, after a cross-burning incident, an onslaught by white fraternity boys, and an incredible flood of rumors about armed attacks being launched against them, also might be terrified. Fear, apparently, is an emotion experienced only by middle-class, middle-aged whites. This strange inability to understand one's fellow man reflects a peculiar form of racism, attributing as it does to Blacks a different kind of humanity from that of whites. As long as these attitudes persist, communication between Blacks and whites at the university will remain difficult.

Although Black student groups have served as the "cutting edge" of campus rebellions, other students and organizations have quickly become actively involved. This involvement, often allying white student groups with Blacks, has created a basis upon which young whites can once again participate as activists in the Black liberation struggle. But this new form of "Blacks and whites" together will be substantially different from what it was in the past.

THE RE-ENTRY OF WHITES: FROM INTRUDING SAMARITANS TO ALLIES

Because of events which have occurred on the nation's college campuses since 1966, the stage has been set for the re-entry of whites into the Black liberation struggle as active, formal, and accepted allies of young determined Blacks. Like Senator Edward Brooke, who has stated that the thrust toward total Black separatism will not long endure, most of us in the forefront of the Black student movement as participants and analysts also foresee a change in this thrust. But unlike Brooke, we do not see any total return to non-violence and an integrationist orientation. As far as both active young Blacks and young whites are concerned, the adoption and use of even more radical and violent means seems certain, unless significant, tangible changes occur in the educational arena. Also, the more radical young white students, in particular, are becoming more aware of the fact that the source of the ills reflected in the conditions and problems faced by Black people lie in "respectable" white, middle-class communities as much as in rural, racist, southern towns. As such, they are not at all sure that they, themselves, wish to remain "integrated" into these communities and are thus much less disposed to attempt to integrate others into them. The present generation of white students, more than any other, is aware of the contradictions and hypocrisies that are integral characteristics of both liberal and conservative "law

Chapter 10

abiding" white communities. Many of them also have decided
that the entire system of American institutional and human
relationships must be radically changed if the society is to be
made "safe" for human beings. And they realize, too, that
this enormous task cannot be accomplished by teaching young
Black children to express themselves by smearing paint on a
piece of paper or by teaching them to read a racist pre-school
textbook in some type of "head-start" program. The educational milieu provides the most seminal atmosphere for the
re-establishment of lines of communication, cooperation, and
coordination between Blacks and whites in their efforts to
restructure the society. But, these Black-white alliances or
coalitions will not be entered into by Black students "across
the board," nor without an eye to the alternative gains to be
realized by Black people through such interaction. Blacks
will still reserve political activities in Black communities for
Black people, they will still demand Black studies curricula
and separate instruction by Black professors and they will
still maintain their own separate organizational identities.
Similarly, in any coalition with whites, Blacks will demand
the right to exercise decision-making authority in political
activities where the interests and future of Black people are
directly involved. Where issues concern more general issues
of change, it appears that Black students are amenable to the
more democratic decision-making processes which white activist organizations seem to favor.

In 1966, after whites had left the inner ranks of the Black
liberation movement, young radical whites turned to assault-
ing the military-industrial complex, the perpetuation of the
Vietnamese War, and the relationships extant between the
educational institutions of America and the political, economic, and military agencies of the society. Unlike most of
the participants in the Black student revolt, the activists in
the white student movement have concentrated on America's
role in the international arena rather than on domestic problems. This is an understandable development, because the

most urgent domestic crises and problems have revolved around issues dealing primarily with the conditions of Black people in urban and rural poverty areas and in educational institutions, and whites now were estranged from the Black peoples' struggle. But as more Blacks have come to see their plight as not simply a matter of racist and oppressive domestic policies and practices, but also as being systematically related to America's international political and military strategies, particularly as these effect the "Third World," the door to cooperation between Black and white students has been re-opened. On some campuses, coalitions have already been established around co-ordinated efforts to ban R. O. T. C., to force the liquidation of ties between colleges and universities and the military-industrial institutions of the society, and to educate and politicize apathetic students.

Taking Cornell as an example, let us examine more specific issues around which Black-white coalitions are likely to evolve.

In the international arena, Cornell University is up to its Ivy League neck in politically untenable associations. Recently, George Champion, Chairman of the Chase-Manhattan Bank, made the following statement regarding the bank's efforts to help ease the urban crisis in America by hiring young Black people and investing capital in Black communities:

> Isn't it time somebody stood up and said business should participate [in uplifting Blacks] because it is the right thing to do—the humanitarian, the moral, the Christian-like thing to do?

While mouthing pious and noble pronouncements such as this, Mr. Champion and his bank continue as one of the largest investors in and supporters of the apartheid government in racist South Africa. Perhaps a brief recounting of the circumstances under which Chase-Manhattan became involved in that country will illustrate how hypocritical the bank's posture is.

From intruding samaritans to allies

March 21, 1960, at Sharpeville, began with a peaceful protest against the oppressive South African pass laws. It ended with at least 72 Africans dead, hundreds injured, the survivors arrested, and the prospect of "working for change within the system" utterly destroyed.

In the Republic of South Africa, the white 19% of the population has total political control over 87% of the land. The remaining land (containing virtually none of the country's natural resources) is "reserved" for the Africans, who comprise a cheap labor pool for white-owned industry and farming. The average per capita income of Blacks is about 6% that of whites.

This arrangement is enforced by an elaborate system of regulations. An interesting example is the Criminal Law Amendment Act No. 8 of 1953 (the Whipping Act) which made a criminal offense of any political act committed "by way of protest or in support of any campaign against any law or for the repeal or modification of any law." Such an offense is punishable by an $840 fine and/or three years and/or a whipping of not more than ten lashes.

All African political parties are banned, as are labor unions. Anyone can be held for 180 days in preventive detention without trial and re-arrested immediately upon release. It is a crime to be in possession of a banned book (mostly books critical of the government or portraying Black people in terms of equality).

But the mainstay of apartheid is in the pass laws. Every African is required to carry a pass book in order to work, move about, or live anywhere outside jail. Failure to produce a pass book is a criminal offense, and half a million Africans are charged with pass violations each year. It is the pass system that enables the government to effectively move and control the Black majority, and Africans consider the humiliating pass to be the "badge of slavery."

So it was that the pass laws became the focus of protest

in 1960 for the Pan African Congress (PAC), a recent off-shoot of the African National Congress (ANC). The PAC leader, a young university lecturer named Mangaliso Robert Sobukwe, sent out a passionate call to action:

> *Sons and daughters of the soil, on Monday, March 21, 1960 we launch our Positive Decisive Action against the Pass Laws. Exactly 7 am we launch. Oh yes, we launch—there is no doubt about it . . . . . Are we still prepared to be half-human beings in our fatherland or are we prepared to be citizens—men and women in a democratic non-racial South Africa? How long shall we be called Bantu, Native, Non-European, Non-White, or Black, stinking Kaffir in our own fatherland? . . . How long shall we rot physically spiritually and morally? How long shall we starve amid plenty in our fatherland? How long shall we be a rightless, voteless, and voiceless 11,000,000 in our fatherland?*

The plan was to march to police stations without passes and ask to be arrested. This was to be backed by a general work stoppage. If successful, the jails would overflow, the work force would be cut, and the government would have to reconsider its policies. The protest was to be non-violent and dignified:

> *Our people must be taught NQW and CONTINUOUSLY THAT IN THIS CAMPAIGN we are going to observe ABSOLUTE NON-VIOLENCE. . . . We are leading the vital, breathing and dynamic youth of our land. We are leading that youth, NOT TO DEATH BUT TO LIFE ABUNDANT. Let us get that clear. We are not going to fight or attempt to fight, insult or attempt to insult, provoke or attempt to provoke the police in their lawful duties.*

Over a quarter million people responded to the call for civil disobedience throughout the country. And at Sharpeville,

From intruding samaritans to allies

a "native location" about thirty miles south of Johannesburg, between three to five thousand massed at the police station on the appointed morning. It was not an angry mob but more like a celebration. Even when the police lobbed in tear gas, the crowd only fell back and answered not with rocks but with songs and the defiant thumbs-up "Afrika" salute.

At 11:40 a.m. another attempt was made to break up the crowd. A few Sabre jets from the South African Air Force appeared and made several screaming low-flying passes over the crowd. But this aerial show only entertained the children, who threw their hats in the air.

The police were formed in a long line between the station and a low wire fence keeping back the crowd. Some had automatic weapons. Others stood on Saracen armoured cars. Two or three Africans climbed over the fence and submitted to arrest. Then without warning the police opened fire and for forty seconds discharged 705 rounds into the terrified people.

The South African Government was to claim that the police were charged by an armed mob: "The demonstrators shot first and the police were forced to fire in self-defense and to avoid even more tragic results." But Dr. John Friedman, senior district surgeon, later testified that 70% of the victims were shot in the back. And that not a single weapon was found.

Africans defied the pass laws and refused to go to work throughout the country, but the passive resistance campaign was everywhere brutally suppressed. For example, the police were turned loose for four days inside the Nyanga "location" near Cape Town with orders to whip every male African they encountered. This they did, smashing and looting as they swept through. "For sheer sadism," wrote Canadian newsman Norman Phillips, "the closest comparison to what happened at Nyanga was when the Gestapo sealed off the Warsaw ghetto and began to annihilate it. Had Nyanga fought back, it, too, would have been wiped out."

Dr. Hendrik Verwoerd, South Africa's Prime Minister,

termed the police work "courageous" and "efficient" and told
Parliament that "the riots can in no way be described as reactions against the Government's Apartheid policy. The disturbances are a periodic phenomenon and have got nothing
to do with poverty and low wages."

Lt. Col. Gideon Pienaar, in command of the Sharpeville
police, told a commission of inquiry that "the Native men-
tality does not allow them to gather for a peaceful demonstration. For them to gather means violence." "If they do these
things," he told Phillips, "they must learn their lesson the
hard way."

The world reaction to Sharpeville was one of revulsion.
Verwoerd was shot by a wealthy white farmer. Foreign investors began a rush to withdraw capital, perhaps fearing a
revolution. Suddenly the South African economy was on the
verge of panic. At this point, a consortium of eleven American
banks, led by Chase-Manhattan, renewed a $40 million re-
volving credit loan directly to the South African government.
General Motors, which operates a plant at Port Elizabeth,
bought full page advertisements in the Johannesburg papers
expressing confidence in South Africa and pointing out that
the available "human resources" would certainly lead to
"greater prosperity." Other U.S. firms said the same, for by
taking advantage of cheap Black labor in a highly industrialized country, their holdings in South Africa return twice as
much as investments in other parts of the world. Objections
are brushed aside with the claim that American support has
a liberalizing influence on the Apartheid regime.

Given the grossness of the contradictions within which
Chase-Manhattan Bank and its officials and administrators
are operating, there is little wonder that students—both Black
and white—perceive a credibility gap between themselves and
the representatives of some institutions in the society. But
for the students at Cornell University, suspicions about credibility are amply justified precisely within the context of their

own educational institution. Again keeping in mind the contradiction between liberal white pronouncements regarding a commitment to the interests of domestic Blacks and their simultaneous support of racism and oppression in South Africa, consider the following facts about Cornell University.

In the Spring of 1968, some Black and white students at Cornell began a campaign to persuade Cornell University to sell its stock in banks which were part of the consortium which had come to the aid of the apartheid regime of South Africa in the early 1960's. Despite considerable faculty and student support for the campaign, the Cornell Board of Trustees voted not to sell. There was but one vote in favor of selling.

The result could easily have been forecast. Eleven of the trustees are directors of firms which have investments in South Africa, and five of these eleven men are members of the Executive Committee of the Cornell Board of Trustees. The challenge to Cornell's investments was by implication a challenge to their own investments. Even to trustees whose firms were not involved in South Africa, the idea that human needs and not profits should sometimes be a guide to corporate conduct represented a challenge to their own investments, both at home and abroad, which they could not tolerate.

Here is a list of Cornell Trustees with business interests in South Africa:

James Perkins, President (now resigned); Director of Chase Manhattan Bank. Chase, through its South African branch, Standard Bank, Ltd. (part of Chase's Standard Bank group), has been in South Africa since 1959. Chase's Standard Bank is the eighth largest in South Africa. As a member of the American banking consortium, Chase's loans to the South African Government kept the racist regime alive during the investment crisis of the early 1960's.

From intruding samaritans to allies

John L. Collyer, *Trustee Emeritus; Advisor to* Morgan Guaranty Trust, *a member of the American banking consortium (see Perkins). (2) Director of* Eastman Kodak, *which has a subsidiary, Kodak (Pty.), Ltd., in South Africa.*

Nicholas Noyes, *Trustee Emeritus; Director of* Eli Lilly and Company, *which has two subsidiaries in South Africa: Lilly Laboratories (Pty.), Ltd., and Isando Dista Pharmaceuticals (Pty.), Ltd.*

William Carey, *Trustee Emeritus; Director of* Tenneco Incorporated, *which holds a 25% interest in a concession off the coast of South Africa where geophysical operations are underway.*

Horace Flanigan, *Trustee Emeritus; Director of the* Manufacturers Hanover Trust Company, *a member of the American banking consortium (see Perkins).*

Robert Purcell, *Chairman of the Board of Trustees; Director of* International Minerals and Chemical Corporation *which has a subsidiary, Lavino South Africa (Pty.), Ltd., in South Africa.*

Walter Carpenter, *Presidential Councillor; Honorary Chairman of the Board of* E. I. du-Pont deNemours, Incorporated, *which has an interest in a fluorocarbon plastic company in South Africa.*

Samuel Johnson, *Trustee; Director of* Cutler-Hammer, Incorporated, *which has an affiliate, Cutler-Hammer Igranic, Ltd., in South Africa.*

On domestic issues, Cornell also is fertile ground for Black-white student coalitions. Although the university has "liberalized" its entrance standards for minority-group students, it still remains basically an elitist university, catering to the educational needs of the higher classes of white America.

Universities, especially the elite institutions like Cornell, tend to function so as to maintain a distinct (although not static) upper class in the U.S. A "good" education is one of the criteria for entry into the upper levels of American political and corporate society. By and large, only those students whose parents have the money, or those who are very, very bright, can hope to gain admissions to the "best" schools—the expensive private universities like the Ivy League schools (which train over 50% of the sons of the upper class in the U.S.). The opportunity to receive a good education is simply not available to the "lower" classes.

The following tables demonstrate how those who attend Cornell University are, for the most part, from upper- and upper-middle class families, that the "best" schools are like a private preserve for children of a man with a good education and position in American society, and that ordinarily all but the most intelligent and exceptional children of the lower classes are excluded from these institutions.

Table 2. INCOME

Annual Income Level	Family Income of Entering Freshmen at Cornell			National Family Income Distribution—
	Arts— 1962*	Engineering— 1962*	All Univ.— 1968	1966
$30,000 and up	17%	11%	7%	about 3%
$20,000-$30,000	16	13	10	about 3
$10,000-$20,000	39	39	43	about 26
$5,000- $7,500	7	11	8	22
$5,000 or less	4	5	6	28

*Latest figures available as of January, 1969. The proportion of families in these categories has since increased. The number of minority and other students admitted under COSEP scarcely affects the distribution.

It is obious from the table that upper- and upper-middle class families contribute students far out of proportion to their numbers in the U.S. That 33% of the freshmen in Cornell's Arts College come from families whose income is over $20,000 is astonishing when one realizes that only 3% of the families in this country earn this amount yearly.

Thus, an elite group of men in occupations which represent but the top 12% of the U.S. labor force sent to the Cornell Arts College over 70% of its freshmen men in 1968 and over half the university's entire freshman male enrollment.

Table 3. OCCUPATIONS

Occupation	Occupations of Fathers of Entering Freshmen Men–1968*		Occupations of Male Labor Force in U.S.– 1960
	Arts	*All Univ.*	
Businessman	36.4%	32.0%	8.8%
Professional	11.9	4.6	1.1
College Teacher or Administrator	7.9	0.8	0.2
Skilled Technician, Architect, Engineer	15.0	17.0	1.5
TOTAL	71.2%	54.4%	11.6%
Unskilled laborers	1.8%	2.7%	18.3%
Semi-skilled laborers	1.1	6.8	22.0

*These figures, of course, include COSEP students

At Cornell it will be issues and conditions such as these that are equally relevant to both active Black and white students that will provide the foundations upon which Black-white coalitions will evolve.

Admittedly, the issues around which these coalitions may emerge will likely be specific to each campus in many instances. However, by taking the format of Table 1 in Chapter 7 as a framework, the over-all orientations and philosophies of Black, white, and negro students can be compared with regard to how these may function as the bases for Black-white coalitions and working agreements. The symbols in Table 4 are identical in meaning to those in Table 1 for both Black and white types.

Table 4. Potential for Black-white coalitions based upon similarity in orientation and political philosophy of white and Black types

Types	Black Social Order		Subordinate Negro Social Order		Dominant White Social Order		Types
	Goals	*Any Means Necessary*	*Goals*	*Means*	*Goals*	*Means*	
Black Radical Activist	+>	+	-<	-<	-<	-<	White Radical
Black Militant	+>	+	-<	-<	+	-	White Ultra-liberal
Black Revolutionary	+>	+>	-<	-<	-<	-<	White Revolutionary
Anomic Activist	0>	+>	-	-	-	-	
Conforming Negro	-	-<	+	+	+>	+>	White Liberals Conservatives

196

From intruding samaritans to allies

Table 4 points out that the white radical appears as a potential ally of both Black radical activists and Black militants. Theoretically, this is entirely consistent with the political orientations of all three types. Each is basically reformist in orientation and committed to the use of means more radical than non-violent, direct action but is short of premeditated violence in efforts to achieve goals. However, while the radical activist may seek a short-term coalition with white radicals, based upon some predetermined and calculated plan of action or program, the militant will usually hold himself aloof from such alliances unless he has no other alternative. In short, he must be pushed to it. There seemingly is little potential for either the radical activist or the militant to enter into coalitions with white revolutionaries. The radicals' aversion to calculated violence, when other means may bring about desired reform, precludes him from such a move, and the Black militant is reluctant to join hands with white revolutionaries (1) because of his need to relegate all whites to the sphere of "outsiders" (the same basic reason for his reluctance to enter into coalitions with white radicals who manifest political orientations similar to his own); (2) because of his unwillingness to become involved in premeditated activities which might act to jeopardize his goal of graduation and individual mobility within the existing social order; and (3) because the white revolutionary, like his Black counterpart, espouses a level of political sophistication and commitment which is beyond the grasp of the Black militant.

The potential for the natural coalition appears to be between the Black and white revolutionaries. They are practically identical in both their domestic and international political orientations; they are both well-read and sophisticated on the systematic institutional relationships that influence American foreign policy and domestic practices—part and parcel of the same network of oppression; and, they are similarly committed to the total destruction of the status quo by whatever means necessary. And they both have settled upon the college campus as the ideal forum for politicizing other students and spurring them to a greater awareness of political issues.

The anomic activist has no discernible counterpart in the white student movement with whom he seems a natural ally. For he is committed neither to a cohesive philosophy nor a delimited range of goal-oriented means. However, it is quite likely that he will be carried into possible coalition with whites through his dependence upon the Black revolutionary for direction.

Of course, the conforming negro has never relinquished his political ties with the liberal white segment of the college community, and as coalitions develop between the other Black and white student types, he may increasingly find himself allied with conservative whites and even reactionary elements on campus communities.

The directions and the potential for Black-white coalitions depend to a great extent on future developments in the academic community. If the problems and confrontations raging in academia today continue to escalate, such coalitions will be inevitable. And depending upon the issues involved and the university's response to student activities, constructive rebellion may turn into destructive revolution signaling the beginning of the total demise of the educational institution as we know it today.

FUTURE PROGNOSIS AND PERSPECTIVES

It was cold and rainy in San Francisco as I watched two little girls standing on the street corner opposite me waiting for the steady stream of fast-moving traffic to slow down or stop so that they could rush to my side of the street. Two police officers—one negro and one white—happened by and, seeing the two diminutive figures with their "Afro" hair styles dripping with cold rain, they stopped their squad car to help the children cross. The white officer got out of the driver's side of the car and stopped the traffic while his partner went over and took the two little girls' hands and led them across the street. A few feet from me, after having made the crossing, the negro cop asked the girls how old they were and where they were going on such a dreary, wet day. They told him that they were each five years old and that they were returning home from their kindergarten class. He bade them goodbye and started to leave when he was suddenly stopped in his tracks by the children's synchronized retort to his farewell: their smiles were wide, and their eyes glowed as they waved and spontaneously shouted in unison, "Goodbye! And thanks a lot . . . Pigs!"

In December of 1969, the Chief of Police in Detroit resigned because, as he put it, "I am simply sick and tired of my daughter's fifth-grade classmates telling her that her daddy is the head pig." The incidents cited above are only part of the evidence that future generations of students on college campuses will be even more rebellious and anti-status quo than the present generation. Seemingly, the educational institutions of America have two chances to avoid perpetual

Chapter 11

conflict and confrontation—slim and none. Today's high school, junior high, and grammar school students—both white and Black—are more politically aware, more activist oriented, and more intolerant of, institutionalized contradictions and hypocrisies than any others in the history of this nation. Already secondary schools have become bastions of conflict and confrontation, and these students will be heir to the legacies of revolt left to them by the present generation of college students. And, it is almost a certainty that these coming generations of college students will not break what will, by then, be a tradition of revolt.

In response to present campus difficulties and anticipated future student rebellions, many state and federal officials, as well as local civic and college administrators, are taking a hard line on campus conflict. In California, 75 separate pieces of legislation focusing upon campus conflict have already been put before the state legislature and 73 of these proposed laws would make campus trespassing, class disruption, and other actions deemed "detrimental" to the college community, felonies, some punishable by as much as five years in the state penitentiary or youthful offender facilities. New York, too, has before its state legislature bills which would similarly make felonies of various activities typically occurring in campus revolts. Even President Nixon and the United States congress have entered the fray by taking hard line stands against campus confrontations and the use by students of coercive tactics to force reform in the educational institutions of America. These efforts will be of little avail. For there is no central organization any longer directing Black student activities. The lesson has been well learned that decentralization of forces and authority is a vital structural component of any liberation struggle. Under such circumstances, there is no *one* leader to be corrupted, there is no *one* home office, the destruction of which could end the stability of the movement. So such repression does not solve problems.

Future prognosis and perspectives

It merely creates more battles and the rebels to fight them. Under the pressures of heightened repression, the apathetic become activists; the radical become revolutionary; the militant become radical; and negroes become Black people. For, when repression increases, its impact not only weighs heavily upon those whose acts precipitated the authorities' repressive response, but also upon those who deem themselves innocent of any responsibility for such acts. Thus, the act of attempting to control rebellion serves to perpetuate the conflict. The logical progression of the Black student movement hence moves from idealism to revolt to revolution at its ultimate extension.

The slim chance that the educational institution in American society has to avoid destruction is by resort to radical and long overdue reforms. This chance is admittedly a slim one due to the factors discussed above and illustrated by way of the Cornell University case study. The alternatives for educational administrators and other academic officials are no longer those of a choice between giving in to a minority of rebellious activists or saving face by taking a hard line stand on issues of coercion and the use of force in the educational milieu. The choices are between the survival of the educational institutions of America and their total destruction.

As of May 15, 1969, 72 college presidents had resigned from their posts in the face of campus rebellions—most of which were led and/or initiated by Black student organizations. Many found that their jobs were not the soft and secure positions which had traditionally been the fare of college presidents. And while high-level resignations in academia more or less clear the air politically and open doors to possible compromise and soften hardened philosophical and policy positions, what is needed today are not quitters and gutless wonders but college officials with the guts and foresight to make the necessary reforms. For, the earlier these are realized, the easier will be the transition for all concerned.

Conclusion

And so, the Black student revolt continues to rage. Ironically the scene of the beginning of the Black student revolt in 1960 was also the scene of the last major campus confrontation at the end of the decade in 1969. But the scenario and script had changed 180 degrees. From non-violent sit-ins in Greensboro, North Carolina in 1960, to the introduction of guns into an already violent Black student revolt at Cornell University in Ithaca, New York and at Voorhees College in Denmark, South Carolina in April and May of 1969, to student/police shoot-outs and sniper attacks upon national guardsmen at North Carolina A & T in Greensboro, North Carolina in late May, 1969, the momentum and strategies of the movement continue to escalate toward outright revolution. Further evidence of the change is the current practice of dropping organizational names such as "Black Students' Union" for more revolutionary titles such as "Black Liberation Front" and "Third World Liberation Alliance." Also, revolutionary organizations such as the Black Panther Party are increasingly setting the standards of politically relevant activity for Black students. And, educational institutions and the society in general continue to search for alternative methods of first stemming the revolt and only secondly of solving the problems motivating the Black student movement.

Black students continue to push for educations which teach Black people to solve the problems facing Black communities; for courses with as great an emphasis upon teaching students how to live as upon teaching them how to make a living; and for professional schools that turn out lawyers with a greater interest in justice than judgeships, and doctors with more concern for public health than private wealth. Until these, among other, goals and reforms are achieved, the Black student revolt will continue to move unalterably toward the realization of the ultimate "R" in the educational arena—Revolution! For the alternatives now are between freedom for everybody or freedom for nobody; liberation or revolution.

But, regardless of whether the Black student movement ultimately gives rise to Black liberation or violent revolution, the students who have actively participated in the revolt have already brought about changes in the athletic arena, the educational institutions of America, and in the general society which were unimaginable by their parents and other members of the society a decade and a half ago. And, the thrust toward change will continue. For, as stated in the first chapter, idealism in the face of oppression inevitably gives rise to rebellion. And, unless one or the other of the forces is totally eliminated, conflict shall be perpetual and will increase in both violence and intensity. Because of this simple fact, sometime in the not too distant future, civil and campus authorities may come to view all Black students as subversives just by virtue of the fact that they are on college campuses. Indeed, if one considers the Report of the National Commission on the Causes and Prevention of Violence, issued June 10, 1969, it would seem that as far as the law enforcement agencies of the land are concerned, that time has already arrived. Much of the blame for such a situation must be borne by J. Edgar Hoover, who has helped spread the view among police ranks at all levels that any kind of mass protest is due to a conspiracy—often communist inspired—to excite and "misdirect otherwise contented people." As a consequence, the report states, the police—federal, state, and local—"have emerged as an independent political power which in many cities rivals duly elected officials in influence. This poses serious problems. For police, just as courts, are [in theory] neutral and non-political. . . . The present police militancy has exceeded reasonable bounds. A democratic society cannot depend upon force and repression as its recurrent answer to long-standing and legitimate grievances. The nation cannot have it both ways: either it will carry through a firm commitment to massive and widespread social and political reform or it will develop into a society where order is enforced without due process of law and without the consent of the governed.

Under any circumstances, there is little doubt that peoples committed to freedom, justice, and human dignity shall survive. And, if revolution is to be the lot of America, once the smoke has cleared, the hate has abated, and the inevitable rebuilding of a truly democratic and free *AMERICA* ensues, among the ashes that were the educational institutions of the United States, surviving peoples shall find that several frustrated, often confused, but always determined and inspired generations of American Black Students once passed this way . . . .

BLACK STUDIES PROGRAMS: CURRICULA OUTLINES

Debate or discussion over whether or not to institute Black studies programs is no longer even relevant, much less fruitful. A thorough and well-planned Black curriculum is indispensable to the liberation efforts of Black people in America and thus to the welfare of America. Establishment negro spokesmen notwithstanding, Black studies programs are designed to investigate and examine the sources of problems faced by Blacks in this nation and to aid in the solution of those problems. The more oppressive the obstacles facing Black people become—the more critical their problems—the more revolutionary the means of removing these obstacles and solving these problems must become. These programs are relevant, for they seek, in addition, to acquaint Blacks with their rich cultural heritage and thus to augment their sense of identity and assurance as a people.

The following three Black studies curricula are predicated on the notion that education must meet the needs and solve the problems of the masses of human beings. The educational institution must function for the people in general rather than for an elite or elitist-controlled groups. The overwhelming majority of Blacks are never going to attend college. Thus, it is the task of the Blacks currently in the nation's colleges and universities to take whatever their educations currently have to offer and put it at the disposal of the Black communities. Being a student is transient; being a Black is eternal and immutable. It is not enough to think Black or even to look Black. One must act Black.

Appendix

These three curricula programs differ primarily in their conceptual frameworks, ranging from the relatively complex offering at Federal City College in Washington, D. C., to the comparatively simple and straightforward course at San Jose State College in California. Under proper direction and control, any one of them can be expanded, shrunk, or otherwise revised to meet individual campus situations.

Black Studies Program / Federal City College / 1968

The Black Studies Program is composed of two major parts: (1) a degree program, (2) a series of individual course offerings.

THE COURSE OF STUDIES

This is a systematic four year course of study which will lead to a degree in Black Studies. It is designed to develop skilled technicians who use their skills—scientific, cultural, and political— for the liberation of African people and the building of a durable and productive African nation. All courses in this degree program are mandatory, (see chart), though the student is expected to begin to specialize in one of three basic areas in his third year. The first two years have as their major focus the decolonization of the mind of the student, and the development of the interpretative skills necessary to define for ourselves the relationship between our history as a people and our present situation so that we may better understand how we must create our future. The total amount of college credits for the completion of the first quarter of the course of study will be 16.

THE INDIVIDUAL COURSE OFFERINGS

The Black Studies Program also will offer several individual courses which will not lead to a degree in Black Studies, but will focus upon various aspects of Black history and culture (see below), and which will be open to the entire student body for credit.

Appendix: Black studies programs

Black Studies Program   YEAR ONE   *(All courses mandatory)*

FOCUS: Decolonization of the mind
Development of the ways of looking at the world
(Interpretative Skills)

Area Courses	Courses by Quarters

1) *Pan African World:*

The study of the historical, social and cultural development of the 3 major African Communities: Caribbean, Continent, Americas

1st: History and Society in The African World
(History and peopling of African world)
2nd: African Civilization
(Literary and Intellectual history)
(Organization and content of the African world, i.e., communal patterns)·
3rd: Contemporary Problems and Prospects in the Pan African World

2) *Natural Sciences:*

Basic Courses—Historical survey of the general principles and uses of the sciences and introduction to practical application of these principles to the social life of the black community.

1st: Uses of Science in History, a Basic Course
(Historical functions)
2nd: History of Math/ . . . of Biological Science/ . . . of the Physical Sciences (ONE of the 3)
3rd: Application and Implementation of Biological Sciences/ Physical Sciences/Math (ONE of 3)

3) *Communicative Skills:*

A course designed to advance the concepts and applications of Reading, Writing and Speech.

1st: Usage of Language
(Role in African societies, a conceptual approach using no single language as the limiting criterion)

207

Area Courses	Courses by Quarters
	2nd: Seminar Workshop in Development of Communicative skills
	3rd: Compositional Procedure (Practical, basic application of communicative skills)
4) *African Peoples and World Reality:* The survey and analysis of the dominating forces and facts and the relationship of African peoples to this context.	1st: Uses and Techniques of Pacification (Moving from a poverty program level to the level of foreign aid in order to develop a world view of pacification)
	2nd: Politics of Dependency (Educational, political, anthropological, economical)
	3rd: Quest for Unity and Solidarity/African Peoples in the Third World
5) *Languages:*	1st: Choice of: Swahili, Kikuyu, Arabic, French, Spanish, Portuguese
	2nd: Continuation
	3rd: Continuation
6) *Physical Development:* Program of study and activity in the arts which strengthen the body and discipline the mind.	1st: Choice of: Akido, Karate, T'ai Chi, Gung Fu, Stick Fighting, Riflery, Aquatics, Gymnastics, The African Hunt, Dance
	2nd: Continuation
	3rd: Continuation

Black Studies Program YEAR TWO

(All courses mandatory)

FOCUS: Major emphasis on Interpretative Skills

Area Courses

1) *Interpretation of the African Experience:*

History and analysis designed to develop the student's interpretative understanding of political developments in the African world.

Courses by Quarters

1st: The African World (survey course)
(Americas, Caribbean, & Continent)

2nd: Imperialism and Racism in Americas. . . . Caribbean/or . . . Continent (ONE of 3)

3rd: Rise of Nationalism
(Federation in Caribbean, Black Power in America, of Independence in the Continent (ONE of 3)

2) *Cultural Concepts of African Peoples:*

Discussion of cultural themes in specific areas of African world.

1st: Black Religion
(Ancestral worship in Africa/Religious movement in Caribbean/Independent Black church in America (ONE of 3)

2nd: Musical Tradition Among African Peoples
(Blues in America / Calypso tradition in the West Indies/Musical tradition in Africa (ONE of 3)

3rd: Literary Tradition (survey course)
(Written and Oral)

3) *World's Great Men of Color:*

Life and Time of.

1st: Nation-Builders
(Sundiate, Musa, Shaka, Toussaint L'Ouverture, Henri-Christophe)

2nd: Men of Resistance
(DuBois, Delaney, L'Ouverture, Walker, Tubman, Turner, Vesey, Toure, Truth, Blyden, Casely-Hayford, John Chilembwe, Bibi Amima)

209

Black Studies Program   YEAR TWO

(continued)

Area Courses	Courses by Quarters
	3rd: Pan African Nationalists (Garvey, Nkrumah, DuBois, Fanon, Carmichael, Forman, Shirley Graham)
4) *Seminars in Developmental Skills:*	1st: Interpretative Skills (ONE of 3) Math/Bio Sci/Phy Sci 2nd: Technical Skills ONE of the above areas 3rd: Applied Skills ONE of the above areas
5) *Languages:*	1st: Continuation of first year 2nd: Continuation 3rd: Continuation
6) *Physical Development:* Intermediate Stage	1st: Continuation of first year 2nd: Continuation 3rd: Continuation

Black Studies Program   YEAR THREE: FIRST QUARTER

FOCUS: After the second year, students will be grouped into one of three cores and concentrated work toward developing particular technical career skills i.e., "major" in Technical Core, Political Core, Cultural Core.

Nation Building

Technical Core:	*Political Core:*	*Cultural Core:*
Training and instruction in the specific skills, scientific and technical, which are necessary to the development of the African Nation.	The exploration and development of social techniques in response to the situation of the Pan African world.	The transmission of the culture and heritage of the African peoples.

Appendix: Black studies programs

Black Studies Program
(continued)

Nation Building

1) Nation-Building: Geography   (required for all three cores)

Technical Core	*Political Core*	*Cultural Core*
2) ONE of three	2) Geo-politics (In-depth analysis of political, economic, social aspects)	2) Cultural Geography
a) Development of Land Resources in the African World (physical scis.)		3) Interpretative Analysis the African Heritage
b) Health Needs and Services in the African World (biological scis.)	3) Analysis of the Political Situation	4) Area Problem: "Who is our Audience and how we reach Them"—the apparata necessary to express truths of the African World
c) The African World and Technology (math and computer sciences)	4) Area Problem: Development of an independence movement—Kenya, Mississippi, D.C., Trinidad (Practical analysis of specific situations)	
3) Specific Problem Study (ONE of 3)	5) Lab	5) Lab
	6) Language (optional)	6) Language (optional)
a) Physical—Problems of agronomy in the Afrcian world	7) Physical Development	7) Physical Development
b) Biological—Tropical diseases in Africa		
c) Math—Develop a math curriculum for African secondary schools		

Black Studies Program YEAR THREE: FIRST QUARTER

(continued)

Technical Core	Political Core	Cultural Core
4) Lab		
5) Language (optional) — advanced		
6) Physical Development		

Black Studies Program YEAR THREE: SECOND QUARTER

Nation Building

1) Nation Building: Institutions (required for all three cores)

Technical Core	Political Core	Cultural Core
2) Developing technical institutions of Pan Africa	2) Developing Political institutions of Pan Africa	2) Developing cultural institutions of Pan Africa
3) Sources and resources of technical development ex: (case studies of AAR, OAY & Guines)	3) Comparative survey of political independent organizations (MFDP, Lowndes County, F.O., CPP, UNIA)	3) Comparative survey of cultural developments ex: (Black writers conf., & Congresses —Jones Annual conf., Paris & Montreal)
4) Lab	4) Lab	4) Lab

Black Studies Program YEAR THREE:
SECOND QUARTER
(continued)

Technical Core	*Political Core*	*Cultural Core*
5) Lab	5) Lab	5) Lab
6) Language	6) Language	6) Language
7) Physical Development	7) Physical Development	7) Physical Development

Black Studies Program YEAR THREE:
THIRD QUARTER

Nation Building

1) Nation Building: Black Thinkers and the Development of the Race (required for all three cores)

Technical Core:	*Political Core:*	*Cultural Core:*
2) Concentration in specific technical training areas	2) Rise of political nationalism—(B. T. Washington—Tanzania—Garvey—Nkrumah)	2) Internal themes—(Back to Africa, vindication, soul)
3) Lab		3) Lab
	3) Lab—Research in technical skilled areas	
	4) Language	
	5) Physical Development	
4) Language	6) Language	4) Language
5) Physical Development	7) Physical Development	5) Physical Development

Black Studies Program   YEAR FOUR

FOCUS: The major emphasis is on the development of areas for the application and acquisition of advanced skills with direction always toward applications.

The fourth year will be a cooperative effort among the Nation-Building Cores on three different levels of:

Individual level
Intra-core level
Inter-core level

within a particular part of the African world

With the shift to a yearly basis rather than quarterly, there must be closer personal supervision between instructor and student.

Black Studies Program / State University of New York at Albany / 1969

REQUIREMENTS FOR UNDERGRADUATE MAJOR IN AFRO-AMERICAN STUDIES

Each student majoring in Afro-American Studies will be required to take a total of thirty-six (36) credit hours within the department. These credit hours are to be filled by following the sequence as outlined below:

(I) A total of twenty-four (24) hours of REQUIRED course work is obtained by taking the following list of courses:

GROUP A   HISTORICAL ISSUES *(Six Credits)*
1) Introduction to Afro-American History
2) Introduction to African History

GROUP B   ECONOMIC-POLITICAL *(Three Credits)*
1) The Economic Structure of the Black Community
OR
2) Politics of Black Power

214

Appendix: Black studies programs

GROUP C   SOCIO-PSYCHOLOGICAL *(Nine Credits)*
1) Tactics on Social Confrontation I & II
2) Theories of Social Innovation

GROUP D   CULTURAL *(Three Credits)*
1) Black Literature

SENIOR SEMINAR *(Three Credits)*

(II) The remaining twelve (12) credit hours can be filled by taking four courses from any of the four aforementioned Groups, three of which must be at the 200 level or above.

(III) MINOR IN AFRO-AMERICAN STUDIES: Any major, who so desires, will be encouraged to obtain his minor in the Department of Afro-American Studies. A Minor can be obtained by concentrating in ONE of the above mentioned Group topics. The interested major will be required to take an additional 15-18 hours (beyond the required 36 hrs.) in the Group of his choice.

Any student from another department who desires to minor in Afro-American Studies can do so by taking 18-21 credits within the Department. Six of these hours must be obtained by taking the Survey Courses in Afro-American & African History.

The remaining credits can be filled by taking any courses from any Group with the consent of the Instructor. Departmental advisors will be available to assist all students in structuring their programs and to insure that all requirements are met.

GRADUATE PROGRAM: DEPARTMENT OF
AFRO-AMERICAN STUDIES

This program is designed to provide the student with an educational and experiential background which is more relevant to the black experience. The program will help supply the student with an intellectual perspective on such vital disciplines as political, historical, economic, and socio-psychological issues that will more realistically enable him to vigorously confront the genocidal forces of racism and oppression. The Department of Afro-American Studies must prepare students for the most complete form of self-expression which must, in fact, be total liberation and self-determination of all oppressed peoples.

TOOL SUBJECT REQUIREMENTS FOR ALL GRADUATE STUDENTS

The student must present satisfactory evidence of the following:

(I) Mastery of ONE of the following disciplines:
   A) Basic reading knowledge of either Swahili, Yoruba, Arabic, Spanish, Portuguese, or Chinese.

   OR

   B) Sufficient mastery of either Akido, Karate, Gung Fu, Judo, Riflery, or Stick Fighting.

   AND

(II) Completion of ONE of the following:
   A) Potentially publishable research and/or creative works which demonstrates adequate sophistication in any of the four major Group areas.

   OR

   B) An internship not less than six (6) months where the student is working in some mode of community activity. This requirement can be met by the student's engaging in such diverse activities as educational, political, economic, cultural and/or social work in the black community.

Possible course work taken to satisfy these requirements is *not* applicable to the graduate degree program.

ADMISSION PROCEDURES FOR GRADUATE WORK IN AFRO-AMERICAN STUDIES

A Master of Arts degree in Afro-American Studies will be offered by the Department. Interested students possessing a bachelors degree will be considered. The department will be particularly interested in students with undergraduate degrees in such diverse fields as: sociology, psychology, government, history, political-science, and other cognate areas. Interested students must submit formal application for admission forms which are structured by the department. In addition to submitting undergraduate transcripts and taking the Morning Session of the Graduate Record Exam, potential applicants will be required to write essays on selected topics to be designed by the department's Graduate Admissions Committee. The final phase of the admission process will be determined by a personal interview of potential applicants by the Admissions Committee.

Graduate students working for an M.A. in Afro-American Studies will be required to take a total of 30-36 credit hours within the department. These credit hours are to be filled by following the sequence as outlined below:

* (I) A total of sixteen (16) hours of REQUIRED course work is obtained by taking the following list of courses:

GROUP A   HISTORICAL ISSUES *(Four Credits)*
1) African & Afro-American History

GROUP B   ECONOMIC-POLITICAL *(Four Credits)*
1) Black Power Politics

GROUP C   SOCIO-PSYCHOLOGICAL *(Four Credits)*
1) Tactics on Social Confrontation

GRADUATE SEMINAR I & II *(Four Credits)*

(II) The remaining credits can be obtained by taking elective courses in any of the four Group Areas, ONLY SIX of which can be obtained by taking 300 and/or 400 level courses within the department.

* Students enrolling in the Graduate program for the 1969-1970 Academic year will be obligated to take the aforementioned required courses.

217

Group A	Historical	Level	Credit Hours

*Introduction to Afro-American History — 100 — 3
A survey of the historical developments of the Black man in the United States.

*Introduction to African History — 100 — 3
A survey of the historical developments of the Black man in Africa.

History of Slavery in the Western World — 200 — 3
A comprehensive study of the institution of slavery and its effects in the Western world.

History of African Cultures — 200 — 3
A study of the major cultures of Africa.

History of the Civil Rights Movement — 200 — 3
The historical development of the major civil rights movements in the United States.

Cultural Geography of Africa — 300 — 3
A study of the Black man in Africa, his regional environs, and their inter-relationship. (Pre-requisite African History).

Pan-African World — 300 — 3
An exploration of the cultural, political, and social bonds among the Black peoples of the Western world (pre-requisite African History).

Black Perspectives on the Reconstruction Era — 400 — 3
A contemporary Black analysis of the political, social, and economic factors relating to the post-Civil War Reconstruction era in the United States (Pre-requisite Afro-American History).

*Senior Seminar: T.C.B. — 400 — 3
The orientation and issues involved in this course are to be mutually developed by both the instructor and the students (Open only to Seniors in the Department).

Men of Resistance in Africa — 500 — 3
An in depth survey of the major Black African revolutionaries, their thoughts and contributions (Pre-requisite Black Nationalism: Africa).

Appendix: Black studies programs

	Level	Credit Hours
Men of Resistance in America	500	3

An in depth survey of the major Afro-American revolutionaries, their thoughts and contributions (Prerequisite Black Nationalism: United States).

	Level	Credit Hours
Pan-African World	600	3

Intensive readings and an in depth analysis of the philosophical, cultural, political, and social bonds among the Black peoples of the Western world (Prerequisite African or Afro-American History).

	Level	Credit Hours
African & Afro-American History	600	4

An intensive survey of the historical developments of the Black man in Africa and the United States.

* Required Courses for all Afro-American Studies majors.

Group B   Economic-Political

	Level	Credit Hours
The Economic Structure of the Black Community	200	3

An analysis of old and contemporary modes of Black entrepreneurship and its effects in the community.

	Level	Credit Hours
Politics of Black Power	200	3

The theories and current trends relating to the development of more extensive and effective control of those political institutions that influence the lives and destinies of Black people.

	Level	Credit Hours
Black Nationalism: Political Perspective in the United States	300	3

The emergence of the spirit of black nationalism in the United States with emphasis on current trends in socio-political and cultural unification (Pre-requisite Afro-American History).

	Level	Credit Hours
Developing African Nations	300	3

An analysis of the contemporary socio-political and economic trends of the developing African nations (Pre-requisite African History).

	Level	Credit Hours
Uses and Techniques of Pacification	400	3

An analysis of the relative ineffectiveness of governmental programs in meeting the genuine needs of oppressed peoples (Pre-requisite Economic Struc. of Black Comm. or Pol. of Black Power).

	Level	Credit Hours
Imperialism and Racism in the Americas	500	3

An investigation of the socio-economic, psychological, and cultural exploitation of oppressed peoples in the Americas by Imperialist powers (Pre-requisite Slavery in Western World, Intro. to Sociol., Intro. to Gov't, or Minority Gruops).

* Required Courses for all Afro-American Studies majors, (Student must choose ONE of these courses to fulfill degree requirements.)

	Level	Credit Hours
*Black Power Politics	600	4

Investigation of contemporary modes of economic and political innovation. Emphasis of the theories and current trends relating to the development of more extensive and effective control of those political institutions that influence the lives and destinies of Black people.

* Required course for all Graduate students.

Group C   Socio-Psychological

	Level	Credit Hours
Dynamics of Racism	200	3

The exploration of the socio-psychological variables involved in the production and maintenance of attitudes of bigotry and racism; their effects and means of change (Pre-requisite Intro. to Psych.).

	Level	Credit Hours
Crisis in Identification	200	3

Psychodynamic analysis of the formation of self-concept and processes of identification as related to the Black experience (Pre-requisite Intro. to Psych.).

	Level	Credit Hours
The Black Family	200	3

The dynamics of intra-familial relations and the effects of social institutions on family life.

	Level	Credit Hours
*Tactics on Social Confrontation: Part I	300	3

(Open to majors only)

A research course in the development and application of techniques to analyze the existing conditions in the areas of political education, housing, and business in the local community (Pre-requisite Politics

Appendix: Black studies programs

Credit Hours

of Black Power or Economic Structure of the Black Comm.; *must* be taken in conjunction with Theories of Social Innov.).

	Level	Credit Hours
Tactics on Social Confrontation: Part II	300	3

(Open to majors only)
Continuation of T.S.C Part I—The application of tactics of social confrontation designed to alleviate the social inequities in the areas of politics, education, housing, and business in the local community (Prerequisite T.S.C. Part I).

Social Problems of the Black Community   300   3
(Open to majors only)
A selective study of relevant problems of the Black community including drug addiction, prostitution, extortion, fratricide (Pre-requisite Dyn. of Racism, Crisis in Ident., Black Family, or Eco. Structure of Black Community).

Theories of Social Innovation   300   3
(Open to Majors Only)
Selective readings and discussions centering on an examination of the underlying patterns of social change; must be taken in conjunction with Tac. on Soc. Confr. Part I (Pre-requisite Pol. of Black Power or Eco. Structure of Black Community).

Doctrines of the Third World   400   3
An investigation of the ideologies and nationalistic bonds of the oppressed Black and colored peoples of the world (Pre-requisites African & Afro-American).

Community Projects   400   3
An internship program where students actively participate in organization work within the community (Pre-requisites Pol. of Black Power or Eco. Structure of Black Comm. & Theories of Social Innov.).

Philosophy of Community Control   500   3
An analysis of the contemporary issues involved in the need for the decentralization of schools, police, and local governmental agencies in multi-ethnic urban communities (Pre-requisite Politics of Black Power or Economic Struc. of Black Comm.).

	Level	Credit Hours
Dynamics of Racism	600	3

Advanced course in the exploration of socio-psychological variables involved in the production and maintenance of attitudes of bigotry and racism (Intro. to Psych. & preferably a course in Personality or Abnormal Psych.)

	Level	Credit Hours
*Tactics on Social Confrontation	600	4

Theories and methods of social change.

	Level	Credit Hours
*Graduate Seminar: Parts I & II	600	4

Two semesters (two credits per session) —orientation & issues involved are to be mutually developed by both instructor and students.

* Required course for majors.

Group D   Cultural

Black Religion	100	3

An analysis of the relationship of Black religion to black culture moving from historical to modern times.

*Black Literature	100	3

A survey course of Black authors, an analysis of their relationship to Black thought and culture.

Musical Tradition Among Africans	200	3

An analysis of the underlying concepts behind forms of African musical expression.

Musical Tradition Among Afro-Americans	200	3

The underlying concepts behind forms of Afro-American musical expression.

African Rhythms and Dance	200	3

A course of study in African oriented and derived music and dance.

Black Art	200	3

A survey of major African and Afro-American art.

Contemporary Afro-American Literature	300	3

An in depth study of works of contemporary Black authors. (Pre-requisite Black Literature)

Literature of the Third World	300	3

An analysis of the expression of a variety of authors from the third world. (Pre-requsite Black Literautre)

Appendix: Black studies programs

	Level	Credit Hours
Black Literature	600	3

Intensive survey course of major African and Afro-American authors, an analysis of their relationship to Black thought and culture.

Explorations in Black Culture	600	3

Analysis of the major forms and expressions of Black art, music, dance, and theatre.

* Required course for major.

Black Studies Department / San Jose State College / 1968

Curricula Offered

This department offers instruction in one major curriculum leading to the baccalaureate degree: Black Studies. The student may elect any one of the following special concentrations: Education, Sociology, Eonomics (All three focus on Black community development.)

Requirements and Procedures

Professional training in this department is offered in the junior and senior years. General Education and Black Studies lower division core courses should be completed during freshman and sophomore years.

Junior college transfers must consult with a Black Studies advisor before registration.

B.A. Degree with a Major in Black Studies

	Semester Units
General Education Program	40
Physical Education	2
Requirements in the Major	30

Blk. Stu. 1A, 1B (6); 40 (3); 100A, B(6); elect. 3 units from the following: Blk. Stu. 110 (3); 120 (3); 130 (3); 140 (3); 150 (3); Blk. Stu. 160 (3); 170 (3); 180 (3) and/or Blk. Stu. 190 (3); Blk. Stu. 105 (3).

Minor or Electives	52

124

Minor Program

A minor in Black Studies is offered for students majoring in other departments of the College.

Semester Units

Requirements in the minor... 15

1A, B; 100A, B; plus 2-4 courses (6-12 units) selected with consent and advice of the departmental advisor from the appropriate upper division courses to be offered by the department.

Limitations and Explanations:

(1) A program should be planned in consultation with an advisor to meet the needs of individual students. (A program leading to the Standard Teaching Credential is being developed by the Black Studies Department.)

(2) General Education courses should be selected with consideration of supporting courses in Black Studies.

(3) A minor program should be considered from a supporting field of study. A minor in an academic subject matter area is required for the Standard Teaching Credential.

(4) For further explanation and guidance, students are urged to consult with advisors or the department chairman.

Description of Courses

Lower Division Courses

1A, B. *Black Experience in the United States.* A—Before 1865; B—1865 to present. Orientation to nature and scope of Black Studies. This course will cover the history of Black people in the United States of America, the unique nature of the experience, the structure problems and potential of the Black community and an introduction to the contributions and thought of Black leaders. Three units.

40. *Black Origins.* A study of ancient African civilizations to the advent of the slave trade with special emphasis on the stagnation and decline of African civilization and political institutions. Three units.

Upper Division Courses

100A. *The Black Community Before 1900.* An historical analysis of the Black community in the U.S. dealing closely with the sociology of slavery and the origin and development of institutions in the Black community. Three units.

100B. *The Black Community After 1900.* An analysis of the important migrational trends of Blacks from the rural South to the urban North with an emphasis of the effects of urban life on the Black community. Also an emphasis on contemporary development in the Black community. Three units.

101. *Black Diaspora.* A history of the dispersal of African people since the 16th century with special emphasis on the Black people of the Carribean, Central and South America. Three units.

102. *Afro-American Music.* Analysis of styles and techniques of major traditions in Black music. A general survey of the development of music from the beginning of the slave work-a-day songs to rock and roll songs and modern jazz from the 1950's to the present. Three units.

103. *Afro-American Art.* A history of the rise of Afro-American art from the 19th century to the present, including sculpture in Africa and Black America, and major styles in Black painting. Three units.

105. *Black Community Health.* A survey course in nutritional and medical care, sanitation practices with emphasis upon proper diet, drugs, professional and non-professional medical care and services. Three units.

110. *Education in the Black Community.* Analysis of the economic, sociological and political foundations of education in the Black community. Aims and methods and important leaders of Black education with special emphasis upon the inter-relationship between the Black school, the Black values and the Black community. Three units.

120. *Sociology of the Black Community.* Analysis of important trends occurring as the Black community becomes urbanized. Traces effect of shifting values and conditions upon behavior in work, education, family, church, government, and recreation. Explores current problems of urban survival and growth. Particular attention to empirical studies of Black communities both small and large. Three units.

130. *Psychology of the Black Community.* Impact of Black society and culture upon personality growth in the light of current sociological and social-psychological studies. There will be emphasis on the role of social inter-action in group membership within the Black community in the shaping of normal and deviant behavior. Three units.

140. *Economic Development.* Analysis of the economic development of the Black community from the slave trade to the present. Economic growth theory will be applied to the problems of Black economic enterprise. Three units.

142. *Law and the Black Community.* An analysis of selected statutes and judicial decisions that directly affect the Black community, dealing with the whole concept of law and justice in the Black community. Three units.

143. *Welfare and the Black Community.* An analysis of welfare services and programs and their effects on the Black community. To seek alternatives to dependent welfare programs. Three units. Prerequisite: Blk. Stu. 105 and 120, or consent of instructor.

150. *Black Urban Politics.* Analysis and evaluation of political activities of Black Americans. Analysis of the Black community power structure changing patterns of leadership influence and decision making in the Black community. Three units.

153. *Contemporary Black Thought.* A study of contemporary Black thought. This course will deal with current ideas that affect the Black community with an emphasis on its constructive development. Three units.

156. *Black Nationalism.* Analysis of the sources of Black nationalism and its nature. The rise of economic nationalism in Harlem in the advent of the Garvey Movement in the 30's and analysis on contemporary nationalist movements. Three units.

157. *Religion in the Black Community.* A history of the formation and development of Afro-American religious institutions (i.e. Christianity, Islam, Judaism) in the Black community and their effect on the Afro-American personality. Three units.

160. *Techniques in Community Development.* To develop concepts and approaches in community development in which human beings can become more competent to live with and gain some control over local aspects of a complex and changing world. Three units.

161. *Black Curriculum; Problems and Design.* Identification and analysis of the special problems associated with the development of a curriculum appropriate to students from the Black community. Discussion of selected teacher problems. Special emphasis will be placed upon planning and development of appropriate work for minority tutorial programs. Three units.

170. *Community Research Methods.* Introduction to research techniques with special emphasis upon those research designs appropriate to the study of communities, laboratory, and field applications of research techniques including methods of gathering and analyzing data. Three units.

171. *Seminar in Social Change.* A survey of the principles, concept theories, and studies of social and cultural change. Analysis of reform and revolutionary movements. Characteristics enhancing and inhibiting change. Three units.

Appendix: Black studies programs

180. *Individual Special Studies.* Special study of some particular phase or topic not covered in any regular course offering. Usually includes an individual research project and field activity. One to three units.

190. *Internship in Community Development.* A supervised placement in practical situations where community workers are employed. These will include community planning, correctional services, community development agencies and others. Three units.

196. *Special Problems in Black Community Studies.* The problems to be selected by the department. Emphasis upon the inter-relationships among Black institutions, thought, literature, and art. Three units.

Index

Index

233